WHEN LIFE ISN'T FAIR

Dwight Carlson, M.D.
Susan Carlson Wood

HARVEST HOUSE PUBLISHERS
Eugene, Oregon 97402

WHEN LIFE ISN'T FAIR

Copyright © 1989 by Harvest House Publishers
Eugene, Oregon 97402

Library of Congress Cataloging-in-Publication Data

Carlson, Dwight L.
    When Life Isn't Fair / Dwight L. Carlson and Susan Carlson Wood.
        p.   cm.
    Bibliography: p.
        ISBN 0-89081-719-7
        1. Suffering—Religious aspects—Christianity.   2. Wood, Susan Carlson, 1963-
    3. Spiritual healing.   I. Wood, Susan Carlson, 1963-   II. Title.
BT732.7.C34   1989
231'.8—dc19   88-7461
                                                                   CIP

Acknowledgments

My daughter, Susan, has added immensely to this book with her wealth of insight and experience with suffering, as well as with her writing skills. She has contributed significantly to all portions of this book, however I have written most of it in the first person for ease in reading and clarity of thought.

I want to thank several dear friends and colleagues who have critiqued this manuscript and given many helpful suggestions.

I am deeply indebted to my niece, Lyn Carlson, for her valuable editorial assistance and my wife, Betty, who has gone through all of this pain and remained, as ever, my strongest support. She has actively contributed to the material in this manuscript as well as spent untold hours typing, editing, and word processing.

****

All incidents described in the book are true. However, when only a first name is given, the name has been changed and incidental details have been altered to protect the identity of the person. The incidents involving my family members have not been changed.

Contents

Preface

Preface

The problem of suffering and misfortune is a ubiquitous one—one which no thinking person can long avoid.

A recent Gallup poll revealed that the most frequently asked question is "Why do people suffer?"[1] Throughout history, man has wrestled with the problem of evil and suffering. Philosophers have put forth their tenets, concluding for the most part that there is no such thing as a concerned and loving God because there is so much evil and suffering in the world. Theologians have wrestled with this subject also, but often they have not fully integrated their doctrine with the realities of the world around them. Thus, religious people frequently have a collection of platitudes that serve them well in health and prosperity, but prove inadequate when they are confronted with the realities of life.

Fourteen years ago, I wrote the following preface to the original manuscript of this book:

> As a physician, I deal with suffering daily. I hear the question "Why?" from both patients and their families, from the religious and the nonreligious, from people in all walks of life. A few respond in a positive, constructive manner, but many more respond in ways that only make their problems worse. Rarely do I find that a person turns misfortune into something useful in his life.
>
> You might ask, "Are you qualified to deal with this subject? You are basically in good health, live in a free country, and have a good job." All that is true, and probably the half-dozen years of chronic back pain, a duodenal

ulcer in medical school, and a brother martyred as a missionary really don't qualify one to speak about suffering and misfortune from the vantage point of intense personal experience.

However, there is an advantage to not having to deal with the subjective bias which would inevitably be present in one who is at the time going through intense suffering.

There is a risk in writing a book like this. I must admit that I have been haunted with the thought, "Will God test me by allowing some misfortune to come into my life?"

Even though the manuscript was finished, I had no peace in sending it to a publisher, so I wrote several other books in the ensuing years. In the fall of 1983 I felt compelled to get the manuscript ready for publication. Instead, I was confronted with living through a nightmare—my only daughter was diagnosed with leukemia, and at one point her doctors gave up all hope.

In the original preface to this book I wrote the following prophetic words:

> This book can help you to face the future whether it should involve pain, suffering, and misfortune or not. So many people avoid the subject in health and then are unable to deal with it in sickness. *It is important to decide while we are well how we are going to respond when difficulty comes our way.*
>
> O. Hallesby in *The Christian Life* says, "Nothing is more important for us to see in the light of the Word of God than sickness and suffering. Let us, while we are well, ask God for grace to *glorify* Him when we become ill. Then

times of illness will never come upon us un-
awares. And then they will never become dark
periods in our life, as they do for most people."[2]

This statement has been tested in the crucible of life
for our family. The basic contents of the original manuscript have stood the test in the furnace of affliction and
so are essentially unchanged. However, new personal
illustrations have been used and a greater depth of
understanding is included. In addition, chapter 9 on
"How God Heals" and Part IV on "Finding Meaning in
Suffering" have been extensively expanded to include
the latest medical research on the subject.

Understanding the reasons God allows suffering does
not take away the pain, but it helps us to deal with it
constructively and to ward off disillusionment. It gives
purpose, meaning, and hope in the midst of intense
sorrow.

It is my prayer that this book will be the right message
for you. As Helmut Thielicke wrote during the air raids
in Germany, "But times of crises are not limited to [war
time]. Sooner or later we all face crises, when we, too,
stand in need of the right message."[3]

—Dwight L. Carlson, M.D.
September 1988

I want to thank my father for the joy of discussing our
ideas and together putting them into written form. I am
also grateful to him for the honor of being listed as a
coauthor, rather than just a contributor. Through him
and this book, God has given me an opportunity to
clarify many of my thoughts and feelings on this topic of
suffering, and it is evidence of how I have slowly worked
through my own pain, accepted many losses, and seen

God bring meaning out of it. My hope and prayer is that God would now speak to many more suffering people through these pages and help them see how they can cooperate with Him in bringing healing and new meaning into their lives.

—Susan Carlson Wood
September 1988

Part I
The Problem of Suffering

–1–

Oh No, Lord, Not Our Daughter!

It was the most exciting and joyous day of my life as I walked my daughter down the aisle before 750 of our friends and relatives. On February 18, 1985, surrounded by uplifting music, it felt like I was floating down the white carpet as her brother, Greg, and my wife, Betty, and I gave away our daughter, Susan, in marriage. In preparation for that Monday afternoon many friends had lovingly adorned the sanctuary and fellowship hall to make it "the most beautiful wedding ever." I believe it was!

After the wedding, many exclaimed, "It was such a happy and joyous occasion!" "It was so worshipful." "It gave love a new meaning." "We've been married 20 years and they inspired us to deeper love!" One colleague who has little use for God said it was an "exhilarating ceremony." When the minister pronounced them husband and wife the audience literally jumped to their feet as one person to give a standing ovation. Hardly an eye remained dry after they said their personalized vows. Susan ended hers with "as long as God allows me to live." Everyone present knew that just three weeks earlier she was lying in a hospital bed with leukemia, not knowing whether she would live or die.

The drama had actually begun 14 months before. A senior at Occidental College, Susan appeared to be in perfect health. Her plans included earning a BA, an MA, and a teaching credential by age 22. Then, a couple of days before Christmas of 1983, an incidental blood study revealed a very low white blood cell count. I feared the worst—leukemia. But a specialist said it was not and followed her blood counts closely for the ensuing month over Christmas and her twenty-first birthday. Then an abscess, a high fever, and even lower white blood cell counts indicated the problem was more than a freak incident that would correct itself. On the doctor's recommendation, we sought a second opinion from experts at U.C.L.A. Medical Center.

As we approached the medical center and university, Susan kept watching the students with their jeans and day-packs casually walking or riding by on bikes. She thought, "I belong with them, going to class. I don't belong in the hospital."

I remember asking the parking-lot attendant for directions to Bowyer Clinic, and he coldly remarked, "Oh, cancer patients park on the other side of the hospital." Though we all feared cancer, having a parking-lot attendant be the first to articulate it devastated me. I recall going to the elevator labeled "Oncology," and with her usual inquisitive mind, Susan asked, "What does that mean?" Betty tried to answer as gently as possible, "That's the medical term for cancer."

As we waited our turn we saw all kinds of cancer patients: some very pale and emaciated, others without hair, and one with a mutilated face. It was an awful place to take your daughter who looked the picture of health.

Whenever I have an appointment, I always bring a book to read, and in the 2½-hour wait, I think I read the same half page 50 times.

Finally, after blood and bone marrow tests, we were called into the doctor's office. In an emotionless monotone, as if he had given the same talk a thousand times before, the specialist informed us that Susan had Acute Myelogenous Leukemia. Leukemia is cancer of the white blood cells. The type Susan had was acute, which means that it comes on suddenly, progresses rapidly, and can be fatal very quickly. Myelogenous refers to the specific type of cell affected. The doctor went on to say there was a 70-percent possibility of remission with aggressive chemotherapy, and if that occurred the duration of the remission may be 12 to 18 months. Ten to 15 percent of patients are "up and about in five years." Susan responded, "Ten to fifteen percent are 'up and about'— what happens to the others?" She then realized the answer to her own question; her face wrinkled up like a prune and she started to cry. From that moment through the next few days, her continual thought was, "I don't want to be dead in five years!" What an awful feeling as parents to watch our only daughter struggle with the horrible news of such an illness. How impotent we felt.

With her blood counts so low, she ran a great risk of infection and bleeding, so the doctor advised immediate hospitalization. But Susan wanted to go home and see John before going into the hospital. That was a solemn night. For many hours she and John sat in the living room just holding each other. In fact, they kissed for the first time after being friends for five years and dating for a few months. The next morning, before we left for the hospital, we had some of the leaders of the church come to the house and pray for Susan and her healing.

On arriving at the hospital, a nurse took Susan into the room specially prepared for her as a patient with a dangerously low immunity to any infection. Strips of white tape bearing the warning ISOLATION in red letters barred the door and directed you to a second door which opened into an anteroom. The sign on that entrance prohibited fresh flowers, visitors with colds, and reminded people to wash their hands and wear a mask. The rules for protective isolation also denied her fresh fruits and vegetables, pepper, yogurt, tap water—anything known to carry bacteria. She followed special procedures for bathing and oral hygiene and swallowed a handful of "gut sterilizers" four times a day. She had to wear a mask whenever she left the room—a luxury allowed only after 8:00 P.M. when the visitors leave and the halls are less crowded. Those walks were encumbered by a Hickman catheter, a small tube surgically inserted into a major artery in her chest, connected to a portable IV (intravenous) pump in order to give her the necessary medications, transfusions, etc. With the Hickman attached to the tubing, she was literally on a 10-foot leash during each hospitalization!

During those hospitalizations Betty and I saw Susan do something she had never done before: She held and even slept with a teddy bear! She had never even liked dolls or stuffed animals! John had given her the bear which she named after him. Betty and I hardly knew John Wood, our church's junior high minister, although he had dated our daughter on several occasions. But two days after her diagnosis he asked to have breakfast with us, at which time he told us of his love for Susan. He had planned to give her an engagement ring for graduation and wanted us to know why he would be at the hospital a great deal.

I was afraid he didn't know what he was getting into and that he would later drop her like a hot potato, as I have known others to do in similar situations. I warned, "John, do you know what you're getting into? She has only a ten to 15 percent chance of being alive in five years. She's going to lose her hair. I'd rather you quiet things down now than build up her hopes and then drop her." He affirmed, "I understand and I love her and I am committed to her." With that Betty and I encouraged him and said we would support him. And so through thick and thin, through losing hair three times, chills and fevers, infections and drug reactions, crises and uncertainties, and a grand total of eight months in the hospital, he was faithful. He was a breath of fresh air for all of us.

John became the master of "creative dating." He had been planning for some time to escort Susan to the

Viennese Night at Occidental College, and they were so disappointed when she could not be out of the hospital in time to go. But John brought a tape of waltz music to the hospital and they had their own Viennese Night. Susan wrote in her journal:

> I don't ever want to forget his coming in with that beautiful basket: red ribbon on it—Martinelli's bottle, crystal glasses—beautiful plates and silverware all packed in cloth napkins, placemats, and tablecloth. I sat in my chair and watched him set it all up—giant grin spread across my face—beaming at him and a bit overwhelmed. He lit the candles and I turned out the overhead light. He got permission to eat pizza in here. [He would have to break isolation rules and take off his mask to eat.] Oh—seeing his mouth eat that pizza! And sharing a meal with someone! Wonderful watching him enjoy the music. More music and then looking through the National Geographic book. We talked—casual, just-being-with-you talk. What fun. Relaxing. A break for us both. Almost forgetting the surroundings.
> Thank You, Lord.

Though Susan spent many wonderful evenings with John or other visitors watching videos, eating, laughing, and playing games, mornings were a different matter for her.

> I know why I feel so weak in the mornings—it may in part be just the usual tired and slow to wake up, but I think that's not the real reason. In the mornings I *am* a hospital patient—*it isn't unreal*. It's lonely at breakfast and still uncomfortable [with the abscess under my

arm]. The bath points out I'm a patient—it's
not a shower and I see and feel my legs and
arms—see the little bruises and spots ... I have
my weird bowel movements. I tangle with the
IV pump. I—myself—change the Hickman
dressing—holding a plastic tube going into
my chest. I wait for the nurse to change the
sheets and to come change the dressing under
my arm. It hurts. I take a million pills. And
sometimes this is all before 10:00. Sometimes I
watch TV. It's quiet, I'm alone with the sound
of the air vent (or whatever it is). And after all
this, I sit in my recliner in robe and slippers (I
HATE SLIPPERS, I WANNA GO BAREFOOT!).
I feel so weak and small, Lord.

Like each to follow, that hospitalization brought some
terrible low points. On one occasion her attending physician said, "In fact there are no cures." We prevented
him from telling Susan that, but Betty and I were depressed for days.

That year we had reason to hope Susan would prove
that doctor wrong, though. During the spring of 1984,
Susan received aggressive chemotherapy during three
separate hospitalizations, each lasting about five weeks.
Yet in the four- or five-week breaks between rounds, she
completed her comprehensive exams and two remaining courses; and she graduated—with her class—cum
laude. In complete remission with no apparent leukemia
cells in either her blood or marrow, she felt perfectly
healthy the remainder of the year. She and John set a
July '85 wedding date, and she returned to Occidental
College for her teaching credential and masters. Our
spirits soared; we hoped God had stepped in and cured
her.

Then in December, out of the blue, her counts dropped.
Over Christmas she hoped it was only a virus and the

end-of-the-term stress, but the leukemia had returned. I remember the New Year's Eve service and young people singing, "Seek ye first the kingdom of God and all these things shall be added unto you." The words seemed a mockery. Susan and we as a family sought God and were putting Him first, yet God was apparently denying her the essential of life—life itself.

New Year's Eve we prayed as a family and again called together friends and leaders of the church for prayer. During that hour tears constantly flowed down my cheeks. But I would look at Susan and, though there were tears on her face, she was often looking up toward heaven singing and praying with a radiant glow. She explains her emotions that evening:

> I felt betrayed by God. A month ago I would have triumphantly proclaimed God's faithfulness and love as I reflected on the past year and anticipated the next. Now He seemed cruel—yet I don't believe God had changed, only my circumstances and emotions had changed. So before Communion I went off by myself to pray and I was reminded of how much Christ had suffered. Realizing He knew exactly how I felt, I thanked God. Somehow, I began to praise Him; a peace filled my spirit completely apart from how miserable I felt. It was irrational, even bizarre. Yet I felt both extreme mental anguish and the greatest joy in worshipping God that I have ever known before or since. Throughout the entire prayer time following Communion, both John and I felt no need to ask anything of God, only a desire to worship Him and sing hymns such as "Great is Thy Faithfulness," "Children of the Heavenly Father," and "The Love of God."

We ushered in the new year with Susan's fourth admission to the hospital for a more vigorous treatment of her now-recurrent leukemia. During this hospitalization her oncologist said, "You know, Susan, even if you get a remission, [the leukemia] is going to recur." Those five weeks proved to be the most difficult time for Susan both emotionally and physically. Ten days of intensive chemotherapy depleted her white count to practically zero; she shivered and sweated through weeks of 104- to 105-degree fevers. Nothing cooled her, not even lying on an ice blanket, a plastic mat with chilled water circulating through it. Her body shook uncontrollably, completely exhausting her. Sometimes the fever was so high that the patterns on the wallpaper would swirl before her eyes, and the nurses would find her carrying on conversations with imaginary visitors.

When the ice blanket didn't bring down the fevers, they prescribed an antifungal drug affectionately called "Shake 'n' Bake." She chose to have it given at midnight, after which she would go into convulsive, teeth-chattering chills. Then morphine was administered to stop the chills and she was wrapped in a warm blanket. An hour or so later she would awaken, drenched in perspiration. Sometimes her soaked sheets had to be changed three or four times a night.

Betty also found this time to be particularly difficult. In a letter to her brother, she wrote:

> We have really been shocked and disappointed that Susan's remission was so short. I guess, and I'm speaking for myself, I really expected that if she weren't healed that she would at least have an average to long time in remission. But it seems that hers has been shorter than normal. From the human perspective it seems unfair and useless. . . . But from the spiritual perspective, there's got to

be some purpose even though there seems to be no rhyme nor reason at this point. Words and songs of comfort seem very shallow and hollow; about the only thing that helps is knowing that others have gone through this and have made it. And God Himself had to watch His Son suffer. . . .

I can now sense again the reality of the fact that Susan has been placed in God's hands. She's half through with her third day of chemo and has seven more to go. This will be a long week. Should God bless us with another remission, there will probably be a wedding as soon as it can be arranged. She and John are so in love. They have a beautiful relationship and I hope they can have some happy months if not years together.

The following are excerpts from a letter Betty wrote to a friend:

Needless to say these days are hard. I find myself going from room to room trying to think of what needs to be done next. I'm sure this is because it is somewhat of a shock to me. But this will pass and I'm trying not to be idle. I guess this is my prayer request. It's easy to just sit and stare into space; but that's not very rewarding; so I'm trying to be useful instead of ornamental.

She then wrote about how difficult it was to deal with the thought that Susan might not live:

In ironing her clothes the other day, I was tempted not to iron them and just put them in the closet. Yet I thought, "No, I want them looking nice for her when she gets out." Then, as I was ironing them it just occurred to me that if she doesn't come home, what will I do with these? I felt guilty for those feelings and so I discussed them with a friend. She said ". . . that's facing the reality instead of denying it." That was a big help. I guess God allows these things to come to mind to prepare us for whether Susan would live or die.

My struggles differed from Betty's only slightly. During this hospitalization I thought to myself a number of times that God almost seemed sadistic. Then one day Susan verbalized a similar impression: "God seems to be playing with me. If God's going to heal me, why did He allow the relapse? And if God is going to let me die, why didn't He allow it last year? I'm not afraid of dying—but why all this chemo, pain, and uncertainty?" One week prayers were answered and blessings poured in only to be followed by some new crisis or complication.

During this time she said she "felt God's presence, but He wasn't saying anything." He was near, but He wouldn't tell her what He had in mind—He wouldn't promise healing. Feeling like God was interested in her spiritual well-being, but not her temporal-physical well-being, the thought of not getting a remission "scared her to death."

While praying together she told God: "I'm so tired of hospital smells, routines, interruptions, inconveniences; but I need to praise You. . . . You tell us You will go with us through the difficulties but You don't tell us what path we will take. You have the power, God. You could just say the word and I'd be healed. I'm afraid my lack of faith may keep me from being healed. But so many are praying, even little kids, and they're also praying for John. Please don't let them down."

At times I wondered if Susan would live long enough to marry John. I further mused, "If we *did* have a wedding—with such a mixture of pain and joy—could I get through it without continually weeping?" But I knew if God were gracious to grant a wedding, I would be there with bells on. And if I cried through it all, that's just the way it would have to be.

During her hospitalization we tried to cheer her up by discussing moving her wedding date up from the previously-set July date, but she kept saying, "Let's not talk any more about wedding plans 'cause I don't know what'll happen if I don't get a remission this time. I just don't want to think about a wedding if it's not going to happen."

The congregation continued praying, asking God to intervene, and within a week she did gain a second remission and walked out of the hospital. Her oncologist said that if she planned to get married she had better do it right away because second remissions usually last half as long as first remissions. Her first had lasted only five months.

The day of her discharge, Betty, myself, Susan, and John were enjoying our after-dinner coffee when Susan surprised us with, "Let's plan a wedding!" So the next morning my wife started the ball rolling. John wanted the biggest wedding possible to "let the whole world know how much he loved Susan." Despite some misgivings about her strength, Susan decided she wanted all the friends who had supported her to be invited. So the following Sunday during our morning worship service, we praised God for answered prayer in giving Susan a remission, and then we invited the congregation to a wedding eight days hence. They burst out in applause!

Every part of the wedding was special. Susan's favorite parts were the music: congregational singing of "Great is Thy Faithfulness," a duet, "The Servant Song," a solo of "The Love of God" during the candlelighting and communion, and for the processional and recessional, "Joyful, Joyful, We Adore Thee" (Beethoven's Ninth) and "Praise to the Lord, the Almighty." But for many of us, their sharing personal wedding vows was the highlight.

John recounted the "Top Eight" reasons he loved, admired, and wanted to marry Susan. He spoke of her warmth and affection, her sense of humor, her intelligence—and inserted, to the audience's delight, "and I'll probably never beat you in Trivial Pursuit." He praised her self-confidence, "something many men don't like in a woman, but something I think is important and I admire in you." He spoke of her beauty—both external and internal. And, most importantly, he valued her love for and desire to know God. Finally, he vowed to nurture his relationship with God in order to be the man he should be, to care for her and love her, and to keep himself for her alone.

Susan told of her comfort in discussing any idea, question, or struggle with John and of her respect for him as a godly man. "I love you for the person you are, and am confident of your deep and faithful love for me; I give myself to you joyfully today. I will strive to make this marriage a demonstration of God's love." She then described how she intended to do that: listening, meeting his needs, supporting and encouraging him, affirming him, and not belittling him or trying to change him herself. "I pray that God would use me as *He* transforms you into the best you can be." Because she trusted his judgment and because he valued her opinions, she knew she could submit to him. She concluded, "John, I promise to be faithful to you and love you with all my heart as long as God allows me to live."

John and Susan then enjoyed nine wonderful days in Hawaii—a gift from friends in the church. It was "a fantasy amidst nightmares." But within 12 hours of their return to Los Angeles, Susan's doctor called, wanting to see her immediately. I had been aware of his treatment plans but had made him promise not to say anything to John and Susan until their return from the honeymoon: He urgently wanted to do a bone marrow transplant.

Throughout Susan's therapy we had been told that a transplant was impossible because she has no biological siblings. In fact, the question reminded me of the fact that we had lost two premature babies and, six weeks premature, Susan had to fight for her first week of life. Though God allowed us to adopt a fine son, he could not provide compatible marrow for a transplant. All my inquiries about the possibility of other people donating marrow were answered negatively. However, with the recurrence we again prayed for God's supernatural intervention and His guidance. In my prayer about the possibility of a transplant I asked that it would be exceedingly clear if that should be a course to pursue. And so with the recurrence, I pushed for the typing, against her doctors' wishes, with the remote possibility that Betty or I might closely match Susan.

The astounded doctor called the evening we set the wedding date and reported that my tissue type matched Susan's almost perfectly —a 1:5000 possibility! So while we planned the wedding the doctors pressured me to get her back into the hospital immediately since successful transplants require the person to be as healthy as possible. I told them the difficult decision would be made immediately after the honeymoon, and we wholeheartedly threw ourselves into the wedding plans. We truly learned to live one day at a time, for we were acutely aware that we did not know what another day would bring.

When the four of us trekked up to Bowyer Clinic after the honeymoon, we listened to a recommendation the complete opposite of the doctor's earlier position. He enumerated all the complications and hurdles that could occur, including death. In Susan's case, a person has a

15-percent possibility of not even leaving the hospital alive. Worse yet is an acute reaction between the body and the foreign marrow. For example, the skin or gastro-intestinal tract can virtually disintegrate.

Nevertheless, the oncologist optimistically summarized, "This time we're treating with curative intent!" Susan felt quite healthy again, and she and John were planning to move into their new apartment the next day. Grimly, she faced the realities of going back into U.C.L.A., into isolation, having chemotherapy, total body radiation, and the potential of never leaving the hospital.

An excerpt from Susan's diary at this time read:

> The fateful day arrived, the return of the nightmare after three weeks of life in fantasy land. On the way to the clinic, Dad related everything he knew about bone marrow transplants. Part of my mind asked questions and processed the answers, but the information didn't really penetrate. There was an element of panic, "I know what chemo is like, how much worse is it with the radiation, too? I could enter the hospital completely healthy, newly married, and die. What if it doesn't work? What if it causes worse damage to my body?" But there was also the voice of logic: "Unless God does a real miracle, the leukemia *will* come back sooner or later, and you will die from it. But there is a good possibility of a cure with the transplant." . . . Most of me was numb, while the rational part of me listened and said we'd do it.

When Susan asked if she could have more time with John, she was told "No—either we proceed immediately with the transplant while she's in remission and feeling well, or forget about it," which medically meant certain death. The doctor had already arranged for her admission in one week and for special funding. The Lord clearly seemed to direct us toward the transplant.

The transplant process itself seems miraculous: First, chemotherapy and radiation literally destroyed her bone marrow. While under general anesthesia, about a quart of marrow was drawn out of my pelvic bone through 150 small holes just below the small of my back. After treatment, this liquid was given to Susan intravenously—just like a transfusion—through her third Hickman catheter. Those cells traveled through her veins and into her bones, where they attached themselves and started to grow. They began to produce mature cells that slowly brought her blood counts back up over her ten-week stay.

In some ways that hospitalization was more difficult than any previous one: methadone given for the pain of radiation burns, weeks of 104-105 degree temperatures, and a complete inability to eat until just before her release. Most of the time she couldn't even read her favorite Garfield cartoons.

Nevertheless, we again saw God intervene with the bone marrow's engrafting, the counts coming back up, resolution of the fevers, and her discharge. Vomiting, anemia, and medications sapped her energy for many months afterwards and infections required three week-long hospitalizations—bringing the tally to eight hospitalizations and a grand total of over eight months in U.C.L.A. Medical Center. Yet Susan's strength is returning. Forty-four leukemia-free months have passed since the transplant. Her counts are now completely normal, though periodic skin rashes still plague her. She has taught junior highers at church, has led a women's Bible study, is exercising, is using her English skills on this manuscript, and is now seeking a permanent job.

As a medical doctor and psychiatrist, I cannot scientifically prove a miracle, but I believe God has intervened. The odds against her being alive today are overwhelming. Computing them would have to include the likelihood of her getting a first remission, getting a second remission, eluding fatal infections, matching my tissue type so closely, and receiving the marrow without a fatal graft-versus-host reaction. The incredibly unlikely outcome we have seen must have had supernatural assistance to come about. In other words, you can call it a miracle.

-2-

Life's Not Fair!

For Roger Bandy, a paramedic with the Los Angeles fire department, October 21, 1984 started like any other work day: He arrived at the station 20 minutes early and carefully checked through his equipment before starting duty. However, the morning was a little different from the normal in that he had forgotten his wallet, so his daughter came by with her fiancé to bring it to him. He gave his daughter a kiss and told her he loved her, something he had done every day of her life.

That evening a call came in for emergency assistance. Upon arriving at the scene of the accident, Roger quickly realized the driver was dead, so he ran to the passenger side and began cardiopulmonary resuscitation. He says, "I vividly remember, with every breath, tears streaming down my face, saying, 'Oh, my God, it's not you,' but it was"—his only daughter.[1] The driver of the other car was drunk. He had just hit another car and in an attempt to leave the scene was traveling at speeds of up to 90 miles per hour when he broadsided the car Roger's daughter was in. He hit it so hard it nearly folded in half, then dragged it more than 100 feet. The drunk driver, amazingly enough, was relatively unharmed. After a backup unit came and took Sherry to the hospital, Roger went over to the drunk driver and would have punched him out if his chief had not physically restrained him. At the hospital, Roger and his wife were escorted into a certain room that Roger knew all too well—he had told many people that their loved one "hadn't made it" in that very same room. Sherry had been dead on arrival.

It was several months later when Roger's chief gave me an urgent call. Roger had obtained therapy after his daughter's death, but seemed to be getting worse. In addition, Roger wanted a Christian psychiatrist, even though he was furious with God. I was under great pressure at the time because of Susan's recurrence of leukemia and hospitalization and was not taking any new patients. I was deeply touched by Roger's tragedy—I certainly could relate to it because we might soon share a similar grief. I was still very hesitant to accept Roger as a new patient because those were very trying days for our family. Though I felt competent in helping my patients, being able to push my own pain aside and focus on their problems, nevertheless there were many times before a session that I had to douse my face with water in hope of removing the evidence that I had just been crying myself.

I did decide to accept Roger as a patient and found him to be anxious, depressed, and seething with anger. He said that he had been a Christian since he was a child, and at one point had even thought of becoming a minister. But his mother died suddenly when he was 15, and he has had little use for God ever since then, at least not in any formal way. So he sat in my office hurling his questions and his rage at God. "Why, God—why didn't you give her three seconds?" he cried. "Why didn't you give her three more seconds to get out of the way of the car?" He was furious at God and felt rejected by Him. Life did not seem fair. In those early sessions he adamantly stated that he would never "accept" what happened and he would never be happy again.

Roger is slowly improving now and credits me with preventing his killing the drunk driver and taking his own life. He continues to struggle with the question of "Why, God, did You let this happen?" And he is not alone. I did my residency in internal medicine at the same hospital where Roger's daughter was taken, and I had to bring bad news to many a family in that same room where Roger had been told that his daughter "didn't make it."

That same question—"Why?"—is asked in tens of thousands of places and thousands of different ways every day all around the world. Who is responsible for the pain, suffering, and death that prevails on this earth? Who is to blame for the scores who are killed by a deranged person with a gun—the tragic slayings from a tower in Texas, a post office in Oklahoma, or a McDonald's in San Ysidro? Who is to blame for the hemophiliac boy who contracted AIDS from a transfusion? What about the innocent children who suffer? In Central Africa 10-25 percent of the pregnant women are infected with the AIDS virus, and in Zambia alone 6000 infants will die of AIDS this year.[2] Do we blame a promiscuous parent, society, or God? Most of the global tragedies we can ignore fairly easily, but touching virtually every family are such things as cancer, strokes, and heart attacks. As a psychiatrist, I hear the same "Why?" from those who have been raped or molested, divorced or widowed, fired from a job or struggling with emotional problems.

Pain has been described as being like breathing gas or smoke in a room: A little bit often feels as bad as a lot.[3] Some individuals spend years in agony when slighted by another person. A high schooler not invited to the prom or a college student not accepted into a sorority may be so devastated that they commit suicide. A wayward child, marital discord, or a promotion that was not granted may seem as catastrophic to the sufferer as the untimely death of one's child, chronic invalidism, or physical torture. Then there are all sorts of "silent sufferers"—those suffering with pain they keep to themselves. A good portion of the people you rub shoulders with everyday would fit into this category—possibly you. Suffering is pervasive and sooner or later we will all be confronted with its whys.

Not only do individuals not have the answer to these whys, but often God is used as a scapegoat. A young couple living in a desert community in California was convinced that God would heal their 11-year-old son of diabetes, so they stopped giving him insulin. They truly believed he would be healed—but he died. Then they were convinced he would be raised from the grave in four days—but he wasn't.[4] In response to this they said, "God led us every step of the way. . . . We feel no sorrow, we feel no guilt. We followed God's will."[5]

Questions and responses like these, in my opinion, reveal the tremendous lack of understanding of God's role in sickness, pain, and suffering. God is not responsible for everything bad that happens in the world. The misfortunes that happen are not God's initial plan for mankind. But before I give you my answer to why good people suffer and why life often isn't fair, let's consider some of the misunderstandings that confuse our thinking and create tremendous turmoil in our lives.

–3–

Who Is to Blame?

The following is an excerpt from a letter my daughter received while she was in the hospital, accompanied by some books on healing:

> Dear Susan,
> You do not know me personally, but I have seen you in church many times. . . .
> I have interceded on your behalf and *I know that the Lord is going to heal you if you just let Him.*
> *Do not let Satan steal your life*—do not let religious tradition rob you of what Jesus did on the cross—by His stripes we were healed.
> I have done what the Lord instructed me to do, but I cannot make you read these [books]; only you can do that.
> Be whole, Susan—spirit, soul and body.
> > In His love,
> > [Name withheld;
> > italics mine]

Picture the situation: Susan is in the middle of a hospitalization for a recurrence of leukemia. The chemotherapy treatments rack her body with nausea and high fevers. Now realize that she is a deeply committed Christian, fully aware of the scriptural teachings on healing and doing her utmost to follow their principles. Is it any wonder that such a letter had the sting of Job's friends' unsolicited advice? When Susan showed me the letter, I asked her if it bothered her. "I tried not to let it bother me—but yes, it did bother me some," she replied.

Later, I learned that she struggled over a month with nagging doubts and fears after receiving this letter.

I am sure that the author was trying to be helpful but, in fact, wasn't. Throughout Susan's illness, numerous other "cures" were recommended to us by people who were also trying to help. We were the recipients of a host of letters and pamphlets espousing various cures and philosophies such as diet and vitamin regimes, the bark from a South American tree presumably with curative powers, and an ointment reputed to cure cancer. Some advised her to remove the silver fillings in her teeth or have the iris of her eyes studied. Some told her to just walk out of the hospital, "in faith, believing" she was cured. Others wanted to take her to a healing meeting, even though she was in the hospital hooked up to life-sustaining treatments and medications. I know all of these people meant well, and by and large they were kind, but their advice often added to our pressures.

The question arises: Why are people, most of whom have never wrestled with a life-threatening illness, so prone to advise others and have pat answers to explain the course to take or the solution to illness? I am sure most of these people feel a sincere interest and desire to help the sufferer. However, I think there are other reasons behind it.

Job: A Case Study

One of the oldest books in the Bible, the Book of Job, offers important insight on the subject of fixing the blame and giving advice. Job was a truly good man, blessed by God with great wealth. One day, the following celestial discussion took place between God and Satan:

> Then the Lord asked Satan, "Have you noticed my servant Job? He is the finest man in

all the earth—a good man who fears God and will have nothing to do with evil."

"Why shouldn't he, when you pay him so well?" Satan scoffed.... "You have prospered everything he does—look how rich he is! No wonder he 'worships' you! But just take away his wealth, and you'll see him curse you to your face!"

And the Lord replied to Satan, "You may do anything you like with his wealth, but don't harm him physically."[1]

And so, reluctantly, God allowed Job to be tested. In rapid-fire succession disaster after disaster struck him— his children were killed, all his earthly possessions disappeared, and he was stricken with boils. Then his friends came to visit. At first they showed admirable empathy—they mourned and sat quietly with him for seven days. But when they could not contain themselves any longer, they started offering their own conclusions as to why Job was suffering and what he should do to remedy the situation.

I think they knew he was more righteous than they, and having such a disaster strike him greatly threatened their own health and security. If Job was righteous and such catastrophes fell on him, what would prevent a similar disaster from striking them?

The Need to Fix the Blame

The same phenomenon occurs today. Dr. Julius Segal, in his book on courageous survivors among hostages and prisoners of war, says:

Many of us find it terrifying to acknowledge that we ourselves may ever become victims. We imagine that traumatic crises occur in other people's lives, never in our own. Psychologist Linda S. Perloff calls this our "illusion of invulnerability."[2]

Eric Cassell, a physician with Cornell University Medical College, made the following comment:

> The sick represent a threat to the rest of us by making us dangerously aware of the frailty of our own connectedness, the thinness of our shield of omnipotence, the incompetence of reason, and the transience of our control over our world.

He goes on to say that we find it necessary to fix the blame for suffering on something or someone:

> I use the word "blame" because that is the sense in which the cause is often sought, not only by the patient but also by family, friends, and others in the group. Did the patient do it to himself? Did it come from overwork or strain...? Is it hereditary? All of these are acceptable reasons. But the one seemingly unacceptable causal term is fate. That something should just happen out of the blue often seems the hardest to accept because that gives evidence of how vulnerable all of us are.[3]

Thielicke captures the essence of this in his statement: "In all misfortunes and catastrophes our deepest human instinct compels us to ask who the guilty ones are. ...And even when we cannot find a guilty party in some great or small misfortune, we invent one."[4]

And so, down through recorded history, men have been more comfortable when they can fix the blame for suffering somewhere.

IT'S GOD'S FAULT

God's the Culprit

One of Job's servants had his own explanation for the disasters that had fallen on Job. He came running with this message: "The fire of God fell from the sky and burned up the sheep and the servants, and I am the only one who has escaped to tell you!"[5]

Job's servant was by no means the last to mistakenly blame God.[6] Many insurance policies continue the practice to this day by referring to natural disasters as "acts of God."

An article in the *Los Angeles Times* revealed that blaming God is a universal phenomenon:

> Now that their environment is going wrong, most of the earth's people, knowing next to nothing about overpopulation, global weather and modern science, look for simple, easy answers they can live with. Most often they seek answers in the sacred and supernatural.
>
> "It is the will of God" is the commonest response whether from Roman Catholic Filipino peasants or Mauritanian fishermen, Arab nomads on the desert or Egyptian fellahin along the Nile, as if God wanted half the human race to starve.
>
> Witch doctors in the African Sahel...say the past six years of severe drought are intended to "punish the people" for abandoning the old tribal gods. Failure to carry out rain-making ceremonies and make the former blood sacrifices, they say, has aroused the wrath of He Who Lives in the Sky.[7]

In like manner, the Cowlitz Indians believed the eruption

of Mount Saint Helens was in "retribution for the dese-
cration of their burial grounds."[8] After the devastating
earthquake in Mexico City in 1985, a survivor of the
earthquake concluded, "God must be angry."[9]

Most of us scoff at the idea of holding rainmaking
ceremonies and sacrificing to the gods in order to prevent disasters. Yet even in our modern society, the
feeling that pervades our hospitals and offices in times
of crisis is that if there is a God, He is responsible for our
calamities.

God Seems to Be Pushing Misfortune Buttons

I once attended the funeral of a young woman who
rejected medical treatment at the onset of a life-threatening illness because she was convinced she would be
healed. But she died. At the funeral, someone remarked
to me, "Isn't it great to know that God makes no mistakes?" By this she implied that this young person's
death was exactly what God wanted.

The belief that God is in control of the universe leads
some people to conclude He has planned every last
detail and wants every event to come about exactly as it
does. Such a god would delight in pushing misfortune
buttons; this god says, "Let's give Mary an 'A' on her
English test today. Let's give Joanne a dent in her fender.
I'll clog up Pat's sink. Joe will get a heart attack, and I'll
give Susan leukemia." Nothing could be further from
the truth. This theology presents a God who is at best,
capricious, and at worst, sadistic. This depicts God as a
cosmic killjoy, toying with human beings. The logical
conclusion of this philosophy is that it was God who
personally exterminated six million Jews in Nazi concentration camps. This view makes God the prime mover
in all evil and tragedy, and in my opinion, it is a totally
erroneous view.

IT'S YOUR FAULT

If You're Suffering, You Must Be Sinning

Yet another universal phenomenon, even more popular than putting the blame on God, is putting the blame on the person who is suffering. Dr. Julius Segal says in *Winning Life's Toughest Battles*:

> Threatened by the possibility that catastrophes can befall good people like ourselves, a surprising number of us decide that victims of misfortune are simply bad people.
>
> Moreover, by stigmatizing those in crisis, we manage to create a safe distance between us and them.[10]

In the Book of Job, over and over again Job asked—about 16 times in all—"Why am I suffering?" His friends were quick to reply that it was because he had sinned. Their basic thesis was that God is just, so when you sin He punishes you by making you suffer. Therefore if you are suffering, you must be sinning. One friend of Job's said to him, "Stop and think! Have you ever known a truly good and innocent person who was punished?" . . . "My advice to you is this: Go to God and confess your sins to him."[11] We can see how Job's friends felt their security was threatened.

Another factor might explain why they felt so compelled to fix the blame: Their theology was that if you are unrighteous, God punishes you—and if righteous, you are rewarded with prosperity and health. If Job was righteous and yet was being punished, their whole theology was put in question—something that was unacceptable to the religious leaders that they were. Better to find fault with Job.

Equating suffering with sin was also prevalent in Christ's time. Upon seeing a blind man, "His disciples asked him, 'Rabbi, who sinned, this man or his parents, that he was born blind?' 'Neither this man nor his parents sinned,' said Jesus, 'but this happened so that the work of God might be displayed in his life.' " Jesus then healed the man.[12]

When this kind of reasoning—if you're suffering, you must be sinning—is leveled in judgment against others, it can have devastating results. Eugenia Price writes in her book *No Pat Answers* about someone in the church who told a mother whose child had died of leukemia, "God *took* that child because [He] demanded to be at the center of everyone's life." The implication was that the mother was being punished because she didn't put God first in her life. The mother ended up in a mental institution. Eugenia Price also relates an incident in which a young boy was blinded in a fireworks accident and a well-meaning Christian blamed it on the supposed wickedness of the boy's father.[13]

Early in my daughter's illness, my family had to face the question of whether or not there was any sin in our lives which might be causing her illness. Susan, Betty, and I were honestly able to dismiss the thought fairly quickly—that doesn't mean we think we are perfect, but we feel we sincerely try to do that which is pleasing to God. However, my son, Greg, had more difficulty with this issue. He was struggling with what many 18-year-olds struggle with—the meaning of life and his commitment to God. Thus it was a confusing time in his life. This made it very difficult visiting Susan in the hospital, seeing people plagued with sicknesses, and it was upsetting to see his sister in such pain, struggling for her very life. And so he tended to withdraw from the situation. From our perspective as parents, he dealt with his tangled feelings by associating with some friends and doing some things we did not approve of.

One night he came into my study very late at night and wanted to talk. He asked if Betty or I had ever wondered if we might have caused Susan's illness by any sin in our lives. I told him we had wondered about it, but had been able to put that question to rest. Then he asked if I thought anything he was doing might be causing Susan's illness.

In a flash I saw my golden opportunity. I could use this moment to coax Greg into a lifestyle more to my liking. In fact, I could use it as a club over his head and tell him to get his life squared away or it might affect the outcome of Susan's illness. However, I resisted the temptation and told him that while his spiritual life did not have anything to do with her illness, God might use her illness to help him think more seriously about how he wanted to live his own life. This scenario illustrates how tempting it can be to use suffering as a way to manipulate people, and unfortunately, it is not an uncommon occurrence.

(For individuals reading this book and struggling with the question of personal guilt, I will give some helps in dealing with this in chapter 8.)

If You Are Good, You Will Never Suffer

The topic of manipulating brings us back again to Job's friends, who were experts at the art. Despite their best efforts, Job didn't react to their taunts of "If you are suffering, you are bad." So they decided to try another variation on the formula: "If you are good, you will never suffer." They told him that if he had lived a good life, he would have guaranteed himself a life free of suffering. In fact, it would have been his ticket to "the good life." They said to him, "If you were pure and good, he would hear your prayer, and answer you, and bless you with a happy home."[14]

It is true that there are passages in the Bible, especially in the Old Testament, that tend to support the view that if you are good, you will not suffer; in fact, God will reward you. God repeatedly promised the children of Israel that if they obeyed Him, He would shower them with prosperity, and all would go well in the promised land of Israel. Conversely, He warned them that if they forsook Him, He would discipline them.[15]

From childhood we are taught that if we are good we will get an ice cream cone, and if we are bad we will have to go to bed early and not get to watch TV. The same basic principle applies when we grow up: If we are bad, the policeman gives us a ticket or even puts us in jail. This principle is believed worldwide. An article aptly titled "Who Believes in a Just World?" stated:

> There is a great deal of evidence, both anecdotal and systematic, to the effect that many people view the world as a just place, where a person's merit and his fate are closely aligned. The evidence is especially abundant with respect to the perceived link between wickedness and suffering.[16]

Roger Bandy, the paramedic described in the previous chapter, was struggling with feelings of deep anger at God. Why was he angry? On the surface, of course, because his daughter had been killed. However, as we talked more during sessions, we found a previously unrealized but nevertheless very real expectation Roger had of God. He felt that if he lived a "good" life and helped others, he and his family would be insured against personal tragedy. And he was furious when God did not keep His side of the bargain.

This assumption that if you live a good life you will be granted immunity from life's difficulties permeates our society. So many people proceed blindly until tragedy strikes, thinking they are immune from disaster because they are "good." Nancy Sawaya, cofounder of AIDS Project in Los Angeles, commented after finding out she had contracted AIDS, "I never thought it would happen to me. . . . I always thought because I was such a good, giving, loving person that I was exempt from this [AIDS]. It wasn't going to touch me."[17]

I have often noticed that many Christians hold an unverbalized, unconscious belief that a dedicated follower of Christ should be immune to misfortunes. I believe that many people serve God, are active in their church, give money, and even go to the mission field in order to buy favor with God. This unconscious belief surfaces quickly when misfortune strikes; the person becomes bitter and may even reject God. I have seen people totally shaken when a missionary goes to the field and dies a short time later. In 1963 my brother went to Africa as a medical missionary. Within 18 months he was killed by the very people he went to help. Some people struggled with Paul's "premature" death. But God never promised that if you do some noble feat He would insulate you from misfortune. God may intervene—at His sovereign choosing—but it is not our divine right to demand His intervention.

The only conclusion that can be drawn from all of this is that the formulas "If you are good, you will never suffer," and "If you are suffering, you must be sinning," simply are not the whole truth. They may fit nicely into the theological frameworks we build for ourselves, but when real human beings with real human problems are plugged into the formulas, the formulas do not always work, and they often hurt the suffering individuals even further.

If You Aren't Healed, Don't Blame Me

A more subtle form of blaming the suffering individual is with some "good advice." The problem with good advice is that it usually has a formula hidden somewhere in it and, as we have seen, formulas can be dangerous. "Here's my formula I want to share with you," the advice-giver says. What is implied is, "If you follow my formula, you will get out of this mess." So it turns into yet another way to fix the blame.

If you follow their formula and don't receive the desired result, inevitably you will still be blamed. Recently a friend of ours developed cancer and was advised to have surgery. Instead she followed the advice of some friends to undergo alternative treatment in Tijuana, Mexico. After months of such treatment she returned home moribund and died in a few days. The response of the advice-givers? "She didn't go to Mexico soon enough." The letter and other advice used to introduce this chapter are examples of this phenomenon. Unfortunately, Susan's experience with self-appointed advisers seems to be the norm.

The person who is suffering is frequently confronted by people claiming to have the solution to his problem. Often this advice is given in such an authoritative manner that it is very hard to question, especially when the recipient is seriously ill and it is difficult for him to think clearly. In certain religious circles, the prefix, "The Lord told me to tell you" is extremely difficult to deal with, especially for the spiritual neophyte.

Here again Job's "friends" provide us with classic examples. One of them said to Job, "This truth was given me in secret. . . . It came in a nighttime vision. . . . I felt the spirit's presence. . . . Then out of the dreadful silence came this voice." Having authenticated his message with "The Lord told me to tell you," he then prescribes this formula: "Go to God and confess your sins. . . . Oh, do not despise the chastening of the Lord when you sin."[18]

Later on in the Book of Job, another friend "became angry because Job refused to admit he had sinned," which is not an uncommon occurrence when you do not accept other people's good advice. Oswald Chambers' comment on these religious friends was the following: "No one damns like a theologian, nor is any quarrel so bitter as a religious quarrel."[19]

The problem with good advice is that there is usually a truism lurking in its depths. Common today are a number of truisms that have *some* truth, but are not the *whole* truth. "God wants you well" and "Prosperity is your divine right" are two frequently quoted ones. The letter quoted at the beginning of this chapter reflects the belief that God inevitably wants you well.

The problem with truisms is that they reduce God to a pat formula. And when the formula does not work, the consequences can be tragic. The following is a sobering example: A patient of mine was not healed when Christian leaders prayed for him. Because this did not fit into their formula, he was told that God could not heal him because he had a demon in him. Although he was a dedicated Christian, this so devastated him that he became worse and needed to be hospitalized. Individuals who blame or give pat answers often inflict the individual already suffering with an additional injury.

Larry and Lucy Parker, the parents of the diabetic child referred to in the preceding chapter, are yet another example of a pat formula that did not work. In their book *We Let Our Son Die*, they write, "Wesley died needlessly, a victim of our imbalance and misuse of the Bible. We mistook presumption for faith, overstepping the proper bounds of God's sovereign plan for our son's life." They go on to say:

> Formulas have helped people to exercise faith for miracles. Yet dangers exist with the general use of spiritual recipes. People tend to work the formula instead of seeking God. Formulas sometimes put God in a box, implying what He will do every time in a given situation. Formulas often elevate man; we have

> finally figured out how God works, making it possible for us to manipulate Him as we please. . . .
>
> Our experience has taught us that God sovereignly heals whom He chooses.[20]

I earnestly wanted Susan to be healed and would have given my very life for her if I could have done so. There is no doubt in my mind that God wants to heal in miraculous ways today. We as a family carefully followed all the scriptural teachings on the subject of healing as we understood them. We fervently prayed, asking God to heal Susan, but to have the audacity to demand that God heal her—usurping God's sovereignty—we would not do. Even Christ prayed, "Not My will, but Thine be done" just prior to His suffering on the cross.[21] The belief that happiness, prosperity, and health is my divine right is, in my opinion, a religious form of our society's self-centered narcissism. Many people believe that if you are not healthy, happy, and prosperous you are either sinning, not praying enough, or you do not have enough faith. This simply is not true.[22]

If we were to look at every miracle in the Bible, we would discover that there is a wide variety of ways God delivers. We would also discover that there are times when God chooses not to intervene supernaturally. For instance, after a few hours of singing praises to God, Paul and Silas were miraculously set free from prison. However, the next time Paul was imprisoned for more than nine years.

Hebrews 11 describes many of God's miraculous deliveries of Old Testament heroes; however, it concludes with these words: "And some . . . through faith received their loved ones back again from death. But others trusted God and were beaten to death. . . ."[23] In other words, sometimes God steps in, and sometimes He doesn't. So we must be careful of not reducing God to a formula.

We must also be cautious of extremes—demanding that God always intervene miraculously or, on the other hand, relegating such miracles to a past age and denying His ability and even His desire to heal today. There are many Christian atheists (so to speak) who believe in God but are not at all convinced He wants to or is able to hear their individual requests. Their theology is "Que será, será; whatever will be, will be." They are pessimistic and fatalistic, not believing in a God who takes an active part in their lives by listening, caring, stepping in, and working miracles. I believe in a God who is alive and active, who hears and answers prayer, but I am convinced that I must allow Him the right to be sovereign. He may choose to reward my faith and my yieldedness to Him by taking away my suffering, or He may choose not to take it away, using it instead to achieve whatever purpose He has in mind for my life.

–4–

How Can a Loving and All-Powerful God Allow Suffering?

From behind the barbed wire of a Nazi prison camp, with the stench of burning bodies permeating the air, three women were discussing the problem of suffering. One was Maria Gratchek, the others were Corrie and Betsie ten Boom. Corrie had been reading her Bible out loud to them when Maria suddenly interrupted her by saying, "And to the mindless, the words [of the Bible] sound so comforting. In this place, mockery."

"God didn't make this place—men did," Corrie replied.

"But He has power; surely He could stop them. Unless, of course, He's a sadist," Maria retorted.

"Oh, no! He's love, all love," Betsie said.

"Then He is impotent! You can't have it both ways, my dear. . . . Your God smells the stench from those chimneys and refuses to do anything?"

Then she raised her mutilated hands in their faces, hands that had been beaten to a pulp by the Nazis, and cried out, "I am Maria Gratchek, first violinist in the Bolshoi Symphony Orchestra. Did your God will this?"[1]

Philosophers have wrestled with this same question for centuries. As far back as 300 B.C., a Greek philosopher named Epicurus stated the basic dilemma: Either God wants to prevent evil but cannot, in which case He is not an all-powerful God, or else He has the power to prevent evil and does not want to, in which case He is not a loving God. Or stated another way: If God is both good and all-powerful, He would prevent the suffering we see in the world around us.

Harold Kushner struggled with this same dilemma in his book *When Bad Things Happen to Good People*.

> I believe in God...but...I recognize His limitations. He is limited in what He can do by the laws of nature and by the evolution of human nature and human moral freedom. ...I can worship a God who hates suffering but cannot eliminate it, more easily than I can worship a God who chooses to make children suffer and die, for whatever exalted reason.[2]

In essence, Kushner concludes that God is impotent.

In the Book of Job, written approximately 4000 years ago, Job's friends dealt with this theological predicament as most religious people do today: They concluded that God is both good and all-powerful, so if someone is suffering it is because he is wicked and thus deserving of punishment. This gets God off the hook nicely enough, but it still leaves us with many unanswered questions, such as why an innocent child is born with birth defects or why hundreds are killed in an earthquake.

Let's look at what the Scriptures teach us about God. First of all, God is good! Innumerable times, the Bible demonstrates God's concern for mankind—His concern which culminated in the sacrifice of His own Son on our behalf.[3]

Second, God is all-powerful, or omnipotent. The Bible is replete with examples of God's absolute power, starting with His creating the universe and mankind. So we believe firmly that God is both good and all-powerful.

However, we must take a closer look at the meaning of the word "omnipotence," what it does and does not mean. The definition often used is that "God is all-powerful and causes everything that happens in the world. Nothing happens without His willing it."[4] The logical implication of this definition is that every minute detail in life is exactly as God wants it to be. In my opinion, this is a misunderstanding of omnipotence. God *is* all-powerful; but that doesn't mean that everything is exactly the way He wants it to be, and it certainly doesn't mean that He Himself causes everything that happens.

Before you react to that statement, hear me out. First of all, let's take the issue of whether there is anything God cannot do. For instance, the Bible says, "It is impossible for God to tell a lie." It also states that God cannot look on sin—He cannot sin. He cannot be unjust.[5] In fact, Dr. Walter Martin says "there are at least 14 or 15 things . . . that God cannot do."[6] It is not that He is weak and cannot do these things; it is because these things contradict His nature and are completely foreign to His character.

R.C. Sproul comes to a similar conclusion in his book *Reason to Believe*:

> Yes, there is something God cannot do. In fact there are many things God cannot do. Reason tells us He cannot be God and not be God at the same time and in the same relationship. God cannot make a square circle or a two-sided triangle. Triangles by definition have three sides.
>
> The point that is crucial, however, is that all of this does not deny the omnipotence of God but affirms it. The point of confusion rests with the meaning of the term "omnipotence." As a theological term the word does not mean that God can do anything. What it does mean is that God does have all power over His creatures. The whole created order is always under the control and authority of God.[7]

In addition to not being able to do things that are contrary to His nature, it is my opinion that certain choices that God has made may bring about consequences that even He cannot alter. Especially after studying Job 1 and 2 and Genesis 2 and 3, I feel that God cannot give man free choice without giving man the possibility of choosing wrong. In other words, God cannot give people the freedom to love Him if they are not free to reject Him. God wanted a love relationship with man, and such a relationship necessitates free choice. Love can't be imposed—we can't compel another person to love. Furthermore, the very nature of a righteous and just God may make it impossible for Him to reward His followers without also appropriately compensating those who reject Him. We can't really know how much we love Him and how willing we are to obey Him unless it sometimes involves a difficult choice, one that includes suffering.[8]

It is further possible that since God greatly desires individuals who willingly love, worship, and follow Him, He had no alternative but to allow Satan to test them with pain, suffering, and misfortune. This is one of the major points taught in the Book of Job. Let me assure you that this does *not* mean God is not sovereign; in the Book of Job Satan had to request permission to test Job, and God allowed it only within very fixed limits.[9]

Recognition of God's self-imposed limitations is the most difficult concept to grasp in this book.[10] Many ardent Christians will have difficulty with this viewpoint. But I am convinced that when someone reads the Scriptures carefully, it can be seen that when God created the world, He set laws in motion which even He chooses to honor. The problem for us is that these laws intersect our lives in the most sensitive areas—in our suffering and misfortune.

God Doesn't Need to Justify Himself

Let's suppose that a number of years ago I was disciplining one of my children when a friend stopped by the house. Before knocking, he overheard me giving my son a spanking. What do you suppose I would have done when I opened the door and realized he had heard what was going on inside? I probably would have explained in great detail why my actions were necessary. We as human beings feel compelled to explain ourselves because of our insecurity and inadequacy. We are afraid of being misunderstood and losing face. But God has no need to justify Himself. Oswald Chambers says, "God is the only Being who can afford to be misunderstood; we cannot, Job could not, but God can. . . . God never vindicates Himself, He deliberately stands aside and lets all sorts of slanders heap on Him."[11] In the same way, Christ felt no need to defend Himself when He stood on trial before His crucifixion.[12]

The fact that God does not need to justify His actions is graphically illustrated in the account of Uzzah. The ark of God was being transported on an ox cart when suddenly "the oxen stumbled and Uzzah put out his hand to steady the Ark. Then the anger of the Lord flared out against Uzzah and he killed him for doing this."

Now, "David was angry at what the Lord had done . . . and was now afraid of the Lord." Neither of the two passages where this incident is recorded gives us any insight into why God did this.[13] It apparently took David about three months to figure out why God dealt with Uzzah the way he did. Only with a great deal of study did I find the law that had been broken: The Levites were the only people who were allowed to transport the ark, and they were to do it by hand; no animal was ever allowed to pull the ark.[14]

Still, it is hard to understand why God punished Uzzah so severely when he seemed to be only trying to help. The point, however, is that God does not need to justify Himself. Even the Scriptures do not explain every action God takes that seems harsh to us. For example, I have had a difficult time understanding why God commanded the Israelites to wipe out all the people living in the land they were to occupy. There are verses in the Old Testament that give a partial explanation—God was at least in part punishing these people for their gross immorality: "You must not insult the Lord your God like that! These nations have done horrible things that he hates, all in the name of their religion. They have even roasted their sons and daughters before their gods."[15] It is still sometimes difficult to understand why the punishment was so severe. But God is God; He has His reasons, and He is not obliged to ask our permission or enumerate His purposes.[16]

Objectivity Is Difficult

When Susan was 18 months old, I had to hold her on an examining table while a doctor sewed up a bad gash in her lip without any anesthetic. It was pointless to try to tell her that giving a shot of local anesthetic would have been just as painful as sewing it up without an anesthetic, and it would have distorted the tissues, increasing the chances of leaving a scar. It was useless to tell her that a general anesthetic was not warranted for a number of medical reasons. I did try to tell her that even though it was going to hurt, it would only last for a couple of minutes, and we were only doing this for her own good—but I doubt that she understood much through all her pain and terror.

I believe this little incident, repeated a thousand times every day, represents God and humanity. God says His ways are higher than our ways, and thus we cannot comprehend His ways.[17] From our limited perspective, our pain makes no sense at all, just like Susan could not understand why the doctor was hurting her. In the same way, a child of two is spanked for running into the street. Likewise, a loving father allows his child to receive a mild burn when the child refuses to listen to his warnings, so that the child learns about hot stoves and doesn't get a more severe burn later. In fact, prior to 1984 if someone had given my daughter a large dose of radiation and toxic chemotherapy, I would have been irate. However, the day came when I not only allowed it, but as a loving father, encouraged it for a greater good. God's allowing suffering does not preclude His fatherly love for us.[18]

In the middle of suffering, reasons often don't make sense. C.S. Lewis wrote these words after his wife's death: "You can't see anything properly while your eyes are blurred with tears."[19] Even Christ, who knew that His very purpose in coming to the world was to die, cried out in agony from the cross, "My God, My God, why hast Thou forsaken Me?"[20]

Our Myopic View

We humans have a very myopic view of our existence. We see everything from a very constricted perspective which focuses entirely on our few years on earth, totally ignoring the endless eternity of our life hereafter. We grasp and shove like two little kids arguing over which one has more pennies, when their father has willed millions of dollars as their inheritance. A thousand years from now when we look back on the suffering we have had in this life, it will all seem so very small. It is like the way the memory of the intense pain of childbirth fades so quickly when the mother holds the baby in her arms, or how my daughter has no memory at all of getting her lip sewn up when she was 18 months old.

In the illustration below the time-lines pictured represent two vastly different perspectives of our years here on earth. If the average life span is 70 years, then according to the "Man's View" time-line we lose half of our allotted existence if we die at 35. However, on the "God's View" time-line, that half a lifetime lost is infinitesimally small, hardly even worthy of note. "For what is your life? It is even a vapor, that appeareth for a little time, and then it vanisheth away."[21]

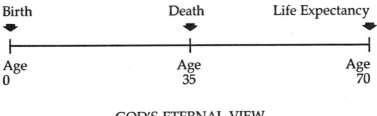

MAN'S VIEW

Birth	Death	Life Expectancy

| Age 0 | Age 35 | Age 70 |

GOD'S ETERNAL VIEW

Birth
Death
Life Expectancy

0 35 70   Eternity
Age

Who Is the Center of the Universe: God or Man?

I have seen scores of people shake their fists at God and tell Him what a poor job He is doing running the universe. A blatant example of this is in the book *Catch-22* by Joseph Heller. The main character makes the following castigating comments:

> And don't tell me God works in mysterious ways. . . . There's nothing so mysterious about it. He's not working at all. He's playing. Or

else He's forgotten all about us. . . . Why in the
world did He ever create pain? . . .

When you consider the opportunity and
power He had to really do a job, and then look
at the stupid, ugly little mess He made of it
instead, His sheer incompetence is almost staggering. It's obvious He never met a payroll.[22]

These statements are based on the assumption that
the world should be run so that man is at the very center.
God is judged by how well He adheres to our agenda. In
our rights-oriented society it hardly even crosses our
minds that the universe might just center around God.

It is not only those who are openly antagonistic to
God who judge Him on the basis of how well a relationship with Him pays off. We who are religious often view
God from a similar perspective. Harold Kushner aptly
verbalizes the internal question in many of our minds:

If God can't make my sickness go away,
what good is He? Who needs Him? God does
not want you to be sick or crippled. He didn't
make you have this problem, and He doesn't
want you to go on having it, but He can't make
it go away. That is something which is too hard
even for God. What good is He, then?[23]

C.S. Lewis gives us a different perspective on this
issue: Who is the center of the universe—man or God?
He says: "Man is not the centre. God does not exist for
the sake of man. Man does not exist for his own sake."[24]
The prophet Isaiah puts it even more straightforwardly:
"Woe to the man who fights with his Creator. Does the
pot argue with its maker? Does the clay dispute with
him who forms it, saying, 'Stop, you're doing it wrong!'
or the pot exclaim, 'How clumsy can you be!'?"[25] A.W.
Tozer says: "Man is born a rebel—He is willing to share

himself, sometimes even to sacrifice himself for a desired end, but never to dethrone himself."[26]

To summarize, the supreme test of a man and his relationship with his Maker comes acutely into focus when a man faces suffering because this strikes at his desire for omnipotence. We desperately want to control our lives, but pain and misfortune reveal our lack of power and our false assumptions about our rights.

(Some of you reading this book are in the midst of deep suffering and pain. Feel free to skip the more theological discussion about the origin of suffering and proceed to the more personal and practical aspects starting in the section "When Answers Aren't Enough" on page 88.)

Part II
The Causes of Suffering

−5−

God's Will and Suffering

When God decided to create mankind, He had the choice of whether or not to give him free will. He could have made individuals without this ability. Then they would always do what He wanted. They would be incapable of sin and therefore never experience any suffering. They would always worship and obey Him, but they would have been robots. As a result, real love—loving someone because you want to—would have been impossible. God wanted people who would love and obey Him by choice, so He created the beautiful garden of Eden and gave Adam and Eve authority over every one of its creatures and plants with one restriction: They were not allowed to eat the fruit of the Tree of the Knowledge of Good and Evil. This exceedingly minimal requirement served to demonstrate their choice of obedience to God.

God told them they would die if they ate from the Tree of the Knowledge of Good and Evil, while Satan told them that they would be as gods if they ate from it. Ultimately they chose to sin. At that moment of disobedience, I believe God had a choice. He could have killed Adam and Eve on the spot and thus annihilated the human race. Such an act would have been entirely justified on His part. He would have immediately administered the proper and previously specified punishment for sin. He would have, in an instant, resolved the entire problem of pain and suffering which has plagued mankind ever since.

However, meting out immediate justice would have prevented Him from finding those individuals who were willing to love and follow Him. God's initial purpose in creating man would have been eternally thwarted. Satan would have been the victor. Executing immediate justice also would have made repentance impossible. So God delayed His judgment. This reprieve, however, meant that the ledger of justices and injustices would not be balanced during man's lifetime.[1]

Thus, for a limited period of time, men could sin without the just penalty being paid. God's suspended judgment of Adam and Eve and of the entire human race forced Him to allow a lack of wholeness in men's lives—spiritually, emotionally, and physically.

Prior to their act of disobedience, Adam and Eve were living in what could be termed the period of *God's initial perfect will*. This was God's original plan for mankind. Everything was excellent in every way.[2] Suffering did not exist. God's desire may very well have been for man to remain in that state forever. However, Adam's and Eve's choice brought suffering and pain into the world, and so humanity entered into the age of *God's permissive will*. Leslie D. Weatherhead calls it "God's circumstantial will"—God's plan operating within circumstances.[3] During this age, God works out His purposes in the midst of and in spite of the circumstances of an evil world.[4] Jesus' comment may well summarize this age: "It was not what God had originally intended."[5]

The age of God's permissive will continues until God chooses to end the world as we know it and judge mankind. Not until that time will the ledger be balanced. Only then will those who have accepted God's provision enter into the wonderful, endless relationship with their Maker. We will live in a world without pain, suffering, or death.[6] The joys God has for us will truly eclipse any sufferings which we have had to endure during our lifetime. We will have entered into the age of *God's ultimate will*—His final will for man.

To conclude: *God is the prime mover in creating life and allowing free choice. He is not the prime mover in causing evil.* He fashioned men and women with the gift of free choice, but along with it came the potential for sickness, suffering, and death. It was our ancestors, not God, who plunged us into this age of suffering.

In the next generation we see a sobering drama depicting the consequences of free choice. Adam and Eve had two sons, Cain and Abel. Both brothers had prepared offerings to present to God. Anger and jealousy consumed Cain because God did not accept his offering, while He did approve of Abel's. Even though God encouraged Cain to repent, Cain killed Abel.[7]

Consider for a moment the fact that God could have intervened and stopped Cain from killing his brother, just as He could have intervened the moment Eve reached out to pick the forbidden fruit. Let's speculate on such an intervention. It could have taken place at one of two points: at the moment a murderous thought first crept into Cain's mind, or at the moment he lifted his hand to strike Abel. At the very moment Cain started to feel jealous and vengeful, God could have made those feelings vanish. That would have made everything nice and neat—no murder would have stained the first few chapters of the Bible. But then Cain would have been in a mental straitjacket.

Let me illustrate such an intervention from my practice. I have treated patients with major emotional disorders of psychotic proportions. Their thinking can easily slip into hallucinations, delusions, and paranoia that can thrust them into suicide or murder. When necessary, strong medications called neuroleptics are prescribed to combat these symptoms. They allow the patient to function fairly normally in society, but there is one major drawback. Many patients complain that they feel like they are in a mental straitjacket; and some, because they cannot stand feeling so trapped, discontinue the treatment, with disastrous results.

Let's look at the second possible point of intervention: Suppose God allowed Cain to think and feel anything he wanted, but when he raised his dagger to kill Abel, God stopped him in midair and an invisible force field shot up around Abel to protect him.

If God did intervene every time we did a wrong, I suspect He would be intervening all the time. If you were ready to verbally attack someone, He would strike you dumb. When you tried to drive your car too fast, a governor would limit your speed. If you overindulged in a Boston cream pie, you would develop lockjaw. Were you about to dig into an unnecessary banana split, it would sour on the spot. If God were to do this to us—stop us cold every time we had the slightest temptation—I suspect we would shake our fists at the heavens. That is, if we could do so. We would be as angry at and critical of Him for that as we are for the suffering in the world. If God controlled our lives to that extent, we would be no more than programmed computers in fleshly hardware.

In conclusion, rather than aggressively intervening in our lives and reducing us to automatons, God chose to create us in His image so that a love relationship would be possible. The logical extension of the account of Cain and Abel is that the righteous can be hurt and even killed by the unrighteous. It is simply a sad fact that a drunk driver can kill innocent people. A mother can beat her crying baby. A man can walk into a McDonald's and open fire on the crowd.

Were the six million Jews who were exterminated by Hitler more sinful than other people? Christ answered this question when He commented on a group of Jews who had been sacrificing at the temple and were butchered by Roman soldiers: "Do you think they were worse sinners than other men from Galilee? . . . Is that why they suffered? Not at all!... And what about the eighteen men who died when the Tower of Siloam fell on them? Were they the worst sinners in Jerusalem? Not at all!"[8] Randolph Klassen wrote the following comment on this passage:

> Here without elaboration or explanation, Jesus accepts the fact that men will exercise their free will for the good or ill of themselves and their fellow men. Some Galileans will choose to revolt. Some Roman soldiers will put down that revolt with the sword. Some will die, some will escape. Jesus recognized that the laws of nature will prevail as when gravity finally pulls down a badly deteriorated tower. God neither waited for those men to walk by so He could push the tower over on them, nor did He send his angels to hold the tower back until these men were safely out of range. He allowed the natural laws and human freedom to take their course. Acts of vicious men, destructive acts of nature—including germs and volcanoes—are not expressions of God's original will. These do not receive His "behold it is very good." They happen under the circumstances of this present age. In most instances, God does not alter these events, He allows them to happen—for now.[9]

Examples of the righteous suffering at the hand of the unrighteous abound in the Scriptures. Solomon, renowned for his wisdom, made this observation: "Some of the good die young and some of the wicked live on and on."[10] Many Old Testament prophets were killed despite their obvious righteousness. The first martyr in the New Testament was Stephen, who the Bible says was "filled with the Spirit," yet he died a brutal death.

Christ's disciples were certainly righteous men, but 11 out of 12 were martyred.

God is not to blame for the suffering and pain that the unrighteous inflict on the righteous. He could make every evil thought vanish into the air, or call a halt to every sinful act, but He chooses not to. He has allowed us to have free choice so that we could be reconciled to Him on the basis of a genuine love relationship.

The Consequences of Living in the Age of God's Permissive Will

Life in this age of God's permissive will brings with it a number of consequences related to the fall of Adam and Eve. The ultimate result of Adam's sin is death. God told them that if they ate of the Tree of the Knowledge of Good and Evil, they would surely die. There was immediate spiritual death. However, out of mercy He delayed their physical punishment, although their bodies began the slow deterioration process that leads to death.

The secondary results of that sin include a curse on the soil, pain in childbirth, freedom to hurt others and oneself, and the psychological traumas of guilt, shame, inadequacy, mortality, fear, and so on. In short, original sin affects every aspect of man's physical, emotional, and spiritual life and contaminates the rest of creation as well.[11]

In addition, Adam and Eve's intimate, uninterrupted relationship with God ended when God expelled them from the garden. The condition the world is in today is a result of this initial spiritual rebellion and separation from God. A.W. Tozer says:

> The moral shock suffered by us through our mighty break with the high will of heaven has left us all with a permanent trauma affecting every part of our nature. There is disease both in ourselves and in our environment.[12]

"Moth and rust" did not corrupt the garden, and no "thorns and thistles" infested the ground.[13] I believe these curses represent the processes of decay and deterioration at work in our world. The physicist calls it entropy: the tendency of all things, if left to themselves, to move to a lower level of energy—that is, to a state of greater disorder. Unless you put energy into your kitchen in the form of tackling the dishes and taking a mop to the floor, it naturally gets more and more disorganized.

During this age, God is allowing the process of decay to continue without His intervention. Not without restraint, however, for then atoms would drift away from one another and chaos would reign completely. God has ordained the laws of nature which help to maintain order in the universe, but He has also established the laws which control deterioration.

Let's consider an all-too-familiar example in our everyday environment. Some years ago I lived in a tract home on which the builder cut a few too many corners. When the house was about 15 years old, the plumbing went out because the pipes were of poor quality. I know some Christians whose plumbing went out under similar circumstances, causing a great deal of damage. They concluded that God personally had made their plumbing go out because He wanted to teach them a lesson in patience. Undoubtedly, God uses the everyday hassles of our lives to teach us patience; nevertheless, for the most part I believe that rust, oxidation, electrolysis, and chemical precipitation made the plumbing go out, not a direct decree of God.

A process very similar to the decay of inanimate objects, like the pipes in my house, works on our bodies and causes disease and death. Joe sat in the front room one Sunday afternoon looking for all the world like the picture of health. Suddenly he was gripped by severe, crushing chest pain. The pain shot down his left arm; he felt nauseated and was sweating profusely. He was rushed to the hospital where they discovered he had had a heart attack.

Did God push a misfortune button? No. Was Joe really in perfect health one minute and close to death the next? Definitely not! Without knowing it, the disease process had been going on for many years. This incident is perfectly analogous to the plumbing problems of my tract home. Coronary arteries deteriorate over a period of many years, developing plaques of atherosclerosis. The first visible microscopic changes have been noted in the coronary vessels of infants who died a few days after birth.[14] Autopsies done on people who died in their 20's reveal that many have significant plaques in the vessels of their hearts, even though they had absolutely no symptoms of atherosclerosis. Only when a greater than 70-percent occlusion develops does the person begin to feel any symptoms. Minute changes accrue over many years leading to an illness that can manifest itself abruptly —on a Sunday afternoon.

This is also the case with cancer. Under the microscope, we can observe the slow development of cervical cancer in women, and only after about ten years is the invasive cancer produced.

The majority of illnesses result from a disease process that was set in motion by Adam's sin with the consequences continuing to this day.[15] With the introduction of sin, C.S. Lewis says that:

> [God] began to rule the organism in a more external way, not by the laws of the spirit, but by the laws of nature. Thus the organs, no longer governed by man's will, fell under the control of ordinary biochemical laws and suffered whatever the inter-workings of those laws might bring about in the way of pain, senility and death.[16]

In a moving testimony just seven weeks after his 22-year-old daughter, Karen, died of meningitis, Thomas Hermiz, president of World Gospel Mission, reflected on the reason why his daughter should be among the ten percent who die from this illness:

> Why did it have to be that way? But we put that question aside.... I simply believe that someplace, somewhere, somehow, nobody knows where or how—and we never will—she ran into a disease that was fatal to her. Fatal it has been to many others across the years. While others have been able to resist it and throw it off, some cannot. Her body was not able to handle that, so she went to be with the Lord. That's all. That's simply life. It's the hard side of life.... God allows some things He does not intend and God permits some things that He does not will. Most of the time the laws of nature are enforced and we will have to live according to those laws.[17]

–6–

Specific Causes of Suffering

Why, then, do good people suffer? Hopefully, the previous chapter has started to give you some answers to this difficult question. I have given background information on the role of free will, choice, a love relationship, and Adam's original sin relative to suffering. In addition, we have seen how *the process of decay, deterioration, and illness causes suffering today*. Also, Cain's killing Abel has graphically illustrated how *individuals are hurt by others*. Let's look at other specific causes of suffering in our lives.

Satan's Role

Perhaps the thought has crossed your mind, "You're putting a lot of the blame and responsibility for the evil in the world on Adam and Eve. What about Satan? He's the one who tempted them in the first place."

A brief overview of Satan's role may help put some things in perspective. Satan was the first to rebel against God. His actual name is Lucifer, meaning "light bearer." He was the most beautiful and honored angel in heaven; however, he tried to usurp God's position and so was thrown out of heaven.[1]

Still, it was not Satan's sin that brought the curse on the earth. The Scriptures seem to indicate that God intended angels to hold only a servant position, while men were to be His friends. It is therefore man who holds the responsibility for the corruption of the earth.

When Adam yielded to Satan's temptation, he forfeited some of humanity's authority over the earth. Satan offered Jesus all the kingdoms of the world if Jesus would worship him. Apparently these kingdoms were Satan's to give, for Jesus did not refute him on that point.[2]

Satan wields immense power. Throughout the Scriptures he uses natural disaster, evil men, sickness, and demonic possession to oppress people. He is referred to in the Bible by such expressions as "the ruler of this world" and "the god of this world."[3]

While Satan may be the god of this world, God is still the Lord of the universe. When Jesus was arrested, He said to the Pharisees, "But this is your moment—the time when Satan's power reigns supreme." However, his power *does* last only a moment.[4] God always limits the extent and duration of Satan's oppression. As Christ reminded Pilate: "You would have no power over me if it were not given to you from above."[5] It is God who remains in ultimate sovereign control over the universe. Satan may hurt us, but he cannot destroy us—unless we let him.

Our Personal Responsibility

Satan reigns on earth. He is the one who sinned first and tempted man to sin. Nevertheless, we must not overemphasize his role. There are two attitudes about Satan that are common today. Christians who have the first attitude look upon every irritant in life—lost keys on Sunday morning, a worn-out clutch, termites in the roof—as direct Satanic persecution. Too often, this serves as a convenient excuse for personal irresponsibility.

The phrase "The devil made me do it!" epitomizes the second attitude. This attitude makes light of sin. Sin is looked upon as a joke, an understandable mistake, or a harmless foible, instead of a gross defamation of God's holy character. In addition, this attitude minimizes personal responsibility. The Bible unequivocally states that the devil does *not* "make" you do anything. It says that

God provides a way of escape from every temptation. Therefore, we humans share the responsibility. Another passage defines temptation as being carried away by our *own* lust—our *own* desires.[6]

Some individuals hold more responsibility for their personal problems than they are willing to admit. Hundreds, if not thousands, of individuals or nations fill the Bible with examples of those who sinned and, as a direct result, were allowed to suffer at the hands of men or the elements. When the Israelites actively worshiped the fertility gods of their neighbors, their enemies devastated them because "Wherever they went, the hand of the Lord was against them for evil, as the Lord had spoken and as the Lord had sworn to them, so that they were severely distressed."[7] As emphasized in earlier chapters, suffering and misfortune do not necessarily indicate an individual's own sin is the cause. Nevertheless, personal misdeeds may be the root of the problem, and we must recognize that possibility.

In addition to obvious sin, I believe that mistakes, poor judgment, and downright stupidity may also get us into trouble and spawn unfortunate consequences. One Sunday afternoon several years ago I needed to climb on the roof to put up Christmas lights. Not wanting to bother getting the big ladder from where it was stored in the rafters, I used the smaller one. While climbing down off the roof, I was looking for the top rung of the ladder with my foot and instead fell, landing spread-eagled, chin-first on the cement driveway. My chin needed 30 or 40 stitches, and I was fortunate not to have been killed.

Now, on whom or on what do we place the blame for this? I have no doubt that my negligence—make that my stupidity—brought on my injury. I doubt very much that I was being punished for any sin or was being persecuted by Satan. I just wanted to save some time and trouble, but the law of gravity continued to be in effect and I fell. Although we might think that suffering from our mistakes and stupidity is not fair, it seems to be an inescapable fact.

Psychological Factors

From a psychological point of view, we human beings inflict a tremendous amount of pain on ourselves. Prior to my training in psychiatry, I was a specialist in internal medicine for ten years. Those years made me very aware of the fact that at least 50 percent of all the illnesses evaluated by the average physician have psychosomatic origins—that is, they are induced unconsciously by a person's own mind. Typically, the person is totally unaware that his own mind is causing the problem. That does not mean the person is not actually sick. It means that stresses from without or within the person's mind are causing the illness. The illness is real, but the initial cause of the illness is psychological, not physical.

If we add to psychosomatic illnesses all the diseases brought on by abusing the body, such as smoking, drinking, and taking drugs, I suspect that at least 70 percent of all illnesses and suffering originate from the individual himself. None of these situations fall under the will of God; none of them are caused by God.[8] But as we will see in chapter 8, even if we are partially responsible for our situation, we have an infinitely loving and forgiving God.

Occasionally God Executes Judgment

Often God allows the natural consequences of sin to execute His judgment, but on occasion He does execute judgment directly.[9] God rained fire and brimstone to punish the wicked cities of Sodom and Gomorrah. He killed Judah's first and second sons, Er and Onan, because of their evil deeds. When Aaron's two eldest sons disobeyed God by offering incense incorrectly in the tabernacle, God sent fire to destroy them.[10] Notice, however, that these were not ordinary men; Er and Onan would have been the Messiah's ancestors had they lived, and Aaron's sons served as the second and third priests of the young nation of Israel, just after God had entrusted them with His laws. Ultimately, God will destroy this earth and execute judgment.[11] God's attributes of righteousness and justice necessitate that there be a recompense for sin. If I had to stop here it would be a sad and pessimistic commentary on God and on the human condition. Fortunately for us, God also has the attributes of love and mercy. Those who recognize God's justice and righteousness, and accept His merciful atonement for their sin, need never fear His judgment.

Part III
God's Sovereignty in Suffering

−7−

God's Responsibility and Purpose in Suffering

When I was in the Navy, I learned that the captain of the ship is responsible for everything that happens on the ship. For example, while the captain is on the bridge, two men can start a fight in the mess hall and one be seriously injured. The captain is held responsible despite the fact that he had nothing to do with the fight. In a similar way, God as "Captain of the universe" is responsible for all that happens in the universe. He created the world with man and his capacity for free choice, even though it was man and Satan who brought out the evil consequences of free choice. God openly takes responsibility for every event that happens in the universe, including all the evil and suffering that falls under His permissive will. God's words to Moses vividly illustrate this concept: "Who has made man's mouth? Or who makes him dumb or deaf, or seeing or blind? Is it not I, the Lord?"[1]

Satan Schemes, God Redeems[2]

You may think I contradict myself when I blame Satan and man for the sin in the world, yet at the same time consider God ultimately responsible for everything that happens in the universe. I can illustrate this apparent contradiction by showing how inaccurately you would perceive a cylinder if you viewed it as only a two-dimensional object.[3] Assume for a moment that you exist in a two-dimensional universe. If you looked at a cylinder from above, you would only see a circle. If you looked at it from the side, you would see a rectangle. We could argue endlessly about the shape of the cylinder if we were only looking at it from the perspective of a two-dimensional being. And why is this? Because we cannot see the whole picture. A cylinder is a three-dimensional object. It cannot be understood from the perspective of two dimensions; it can only be understood from the perspective of three dimensions.

Our view of suffering is as limited as our description of a cylinder in only two dimensions. We cannot see the "third dimension" in which God is working out His sovereign purposes. Every difficulty and evil occurrence has a celestial "third dimension" in which both Satan and God are working. Concealed from us, Satan devises evil and God brings to fruition His redemptive purposes.

Though man's evil actions have none of God's favor, He will turn all evil into good if we permit Him.[4] Let me make this very clear—I do not believe God ever wanted evil, sin, or suffering to plague our lives. But despite man's choice to be disobedient, God continues to work to achieve His ultimate purposes instead of giving up on us. "For everything serves [God's] plans."[5]

My brother Paul was a medical missionary serving the African people in a remote corner of Congo (now Zaire) when rebel forces approached his hospital. He had evacuated his family, but because of his concern for the well-being of the patients, he returned to care for them. After being captured by the rebel troops, he wrote:

> I was wrong to try to stay but I feel I put it all into God's hands and must leave it there. I have learned with the apostle Paul, "For me to live is Christ and to die is gain." [In other words: If I live, it will be to live as a Christian. But if I die, I will be with Christ.] We thought that that time had come several times during

> the last week. We have seen beatings, but God
> is always gracious. I am in good health with-
> out injury of consequence. . . . Pray not for
> deliverance but for my testimony. That's why I
> am here. . . . Remember the church never grows
> in plenty but in time of martyrdom.

And though Paul was ultimately killed, God used this "evil" to profoundly affect numerous lives. Individuals have become reconciled to God, others have gone to the mission fields, and the Paul Carlson Medical Program has been established to continue Paul's dream for meeting many of the physical and spiritual needs of Zaire through a hospital, agriculture, and a cattle program.

For an excellent example of God's redemption of evil, look at Joseph, who was sold into slavery by his jealous brothers. During the 12 or more years he was enslaved and imprisoned, God's purposes were, no doubt, impossible for him to see. Only after the fact could Joseph see that God had used his suffering to save Joseph's family. Only then could he say, "God turned into good what you meant for evil, for he brought me to this high position I have today so that I could save the lives of many people."[6]

I have referred to the cosmic battle between Satan and God over Job. When God declared to Satan that Job was a righteous man, Satan scoffed, "Why shouldn't he, when you pay him so well? . . . You have always protected him and his home and his property from all harm. You have prospered everything he does—look how rich he is! No wonder he 'worships' you! But just take away his wealth, and you'll see him curse you to your face!"[7] Satan received permission to inflict Job with multiple kinds of suffering: loss of his children, material wealth, and position; illness; and criticism. Thus, Satan schemed. However, because of Job's faithfulness to God, we see both Job and God vindicated. Ultimately Job was blessed with twice the prosperity he started with. Thus, God redeemed.

The most awesome illustration of God's bringing good out of evil is the crucifixion. Satan thought he would triumph over God by destroying Christ. Satan, Judas, Pilate, the Pharisees, and the mob that cried out "Crucify him!" were fully responsible for Christ's crucifixion. God allowed Christ to suffer the most painful, torturous death known to the Roman world, but through this death He worked out His eternal plan for mankind. In this we clearly see Satan's evil purposes and God's redemptive purposes, as well as God's ultimate expression of love and mercy to mankind.

God's Purpose in Suffering

Thomas Hermiz, referred to earlier, musing about his daughter's death, said: "Why did it have to be that way?" But he was able to quickly put that question aside and ask, "Lord, what can we learn from this?"[8]

When we suffer, the single most important ingredient is seeing purpose in it. Lack of purpose breeds hopelessness; purpose imparts the strength to sustain. Viktor Frankl, a Viennese psychiatrist, wrote the following about his grim years in Auschwitz:

> Any attempt to restore a man's inner strength in the camp had first to succeed in showing him some future goal. Nietzsche's words, "He who has a *why* to live for can bear with almost any *how*," could be the guiding motto. . . . Whenever there was an opportunity for it, one had to give them a *why*—an aim—for their lives, in order to strengthen them to bear the terrible *how* of their existence. Woe to him who saw no more sense in his life, no aim, no purpose, and therefore no point in carrying on.

He concludes with these powerful words:

> Suffering ceases to be suffering in some way
> at the moment it finds a meaning.[9]

Paul wrote the following to the Thessalonian church during a time of intense persecution: "We are happy to tell other churches about your patience and complete faith in God, in spite of all the crushing troubles and hardships you are going through . . . for he is using your sufferings to make you ready for his kingdom."[10] Scripture indicates that God takes our "troubles and hardships" and turns them to positive use—He redeems them. Romans 8:28 says it succinctly: "And we know that God causes all things to work together for good to those who love God, to those who are called according to His purpose."[11]

One writer says: "To suffer is one thing, to suffer without meaning is another, but to suffer and choose not to press for any meaning is different again."[12]

When we are going through difficulties, it is rare for the sufferer to see the meaning in it. Douglas Webster in *A Passion for Christ*, describes my brother's and other missionaries' "seemingly accidental circumstances." Their deaths must be interpreted beyond the circumstances to discover their meaning. He goes on to state that "There is nothing heroic about the Cross. . . . Jesus appears as the victim of circumstances—a friend betrays him, popular sentiment turns against him, a ruler concerned only with political expediency hears his case, and his disciples abandon him." From the human perspective, this was a disaster without meaning. However, "God infuses the Cross with meaning. . . ."

There are many ways in which God gives meaning to suffering. The following briefly summarizes some of these purposes.

SEVEN OF GOD'S REDEMPTIVE
USES OF SUFFERING

To Get Our Attention

Roger Bandy, the paramedic whose daughter was killed by a drunk driver, told me one day in a session, "The average person takes life for granted; I did until Sherry's death." Unfortunately, most of us do not look up until we are flat on our backs. It has been said that God is heard as a whisper in pleasure; He speaks in work; and He shouts in suffering. C.S. Lewis calls pain God's "megaphone to rouse a deaf world."[14] After spending seven years as a POW in North Vietnam, Howard Rutledge wrote, "It took prison to show me how empty life is without God."[15] The Bible rightly states, "He delivers by distress! This makes them listen to him!"[16]

To Atone for Sin

A righteous and just God must recompense persistent sin with punishment. This is a difficult concept for us mortals to fully comprehend, and elaboration on it lies beyond the scope of this book.[17] Fortunately, it is not His will that any of us should be punished because of sin for which Christ has already atoned and paid the price. More will be said on this subject shortly.

To Give Us the Opportunity to Be Reconciled to God

Fortunately for us, God's character not only includes justice but also phenomenal love. The highest expression of His love was the sacrifice of His Son: "For God so loved the world, that He gave His only begotten Son, that whoever believes in Him should not perish, but have eternal life."[18]

A major reason God does not end pain and suffering by bringing this evil world to a screeching halt is to give people the opportunity to be reconciled to Him and to have the eternal life for which Christ died. "But he is waiting, for the good reason that he is not willing that any should perish, and he is giving more time for sinners to repent."[19]

To Build Character

Athletes often say "no pain, no gain." To be honest, I am not very fond of that statement—I wish it didn't need to be that way. But as I see the weight lifters straining and sweating and marathon runners stumbling to the finish line, there seems to be no way around the fact that there is a lot of hard work involved in any great achievement. It would be nice if our spiritual growth could be without any pain, but that does not seem to be the way it is.[20]

A patient of mine who was going through some difficulties once made the statement that God puts problems in front of us. I'm not sure this is true. Our fallen nature and the world around us create enough difficulties in themselves to build character in our lives. Instead, I believe God is in heaven rooting for us to handle problems well.[21]

The Scriptures frequently state that the trials and difficulties that come our way are used to refine us. Gold becomes more valuable as it is refined by burning off the impurities. In the same way, God works through suffering to purify our lives.[22] Sometimes we need to be purified because of sin. At other times there may not be any sin in our lives; yet God may be using suffering to develop character in us. This does not mean that the person undergoing difficulty necessarily has a greater need for refining than his neighbor with a troublefree life. Nevertheless, God may allow trials, not to correct us, but to perfect us. According to the Scriptures, suffering produces character distinguished by patience, obedience, trust, hope, grace, and faith.[23]

To Teach Us How to Help Others Who Are Suffering

God also uses suffering to make us more sensitive to others. We are better able to point them to God and to be a comfort to the afflicted. The Scriptures say: "What a wonderful God we have—he is the Father of our Lord Jesus Christ, the source of every mercy, and the one who so wonderfully comforts and strengthens us in our hardships and trials. And why does he do this? So that when others are troubled, needing our sympathy and encouragement, we can pass on to them this same help and comfort God has given us."[24]

To Affirm Our Love For God

Yet another purpose of suffering is for us to affirm our love for God. Just as a father shows his love for his children when he risks his life to save them in a fire, so we likewise show our love for God when difficulty comes our way and we remain true to Him. The entire Book of Job is an illustration of this truth. Job remained true to God even in the face of intense suffering. Even when his wife told him to "curse God, and die," Job still said, "Though he slay me, yet will I trust in him."[25]

C.S. Lewis put it this way: "You never know how much you really believe anything until its truth or falsehood becomes a matter of life and death to you. . . . Only a real risk tests the reality of a belief."[26]

To Glorify God

While it was not God's initial will for evil and suffering to enter into the world, since evil and suffering do exist now, God will use them to glorify Himself. He will intervene in despicable situations in order to demonstrate His power, and thus bring glory to His Name. In the Gospel of John we read about Jesus' friend Lazarus becoming ill, dying, and being raised from the dead. Christ's response when He heard about the sickness was, "The purpose of his illness is not death, but for the glory of God. I, the Son of God, will receive glory from this situation."[27] So, sometimes God glorifies Himself through His miraculous intervention. In many other instances, though, He is glorified in the way a person endures the suffering.

Examples of God's Purposes in Suffering

History is replete with examples of horrible suffering which ultimately God used in positive ways. Stephen, in A.D. 34, was the first martyr, and though he did not live long enough to see any good come from his stoning, the greatest preacher of all time, Paul, was profoundly influenced by him.[28]

Foxe's Book of Martyrs depicts on its 370 pages gruesome tortures of thousands of Christians who chose to suffer rather than to renounce Christ. Because of their blood, Christianity grew mightily on this earth.[29]

After John Milton became blind he wrote his greatest pieces of literature: *Paradise Lost* and *Paradise Regained*. George Handel was paralyzed and had creditors threatening him with imprisonment when he composed *The Messiah*.

Because of his faith, John Bunyan was thrown in prison where he was often cold and hungry; there he wrote the masterpiece that has influenced millions, *The Pilgrim's Progress*.[30] Every decade of history knew people who discovered purpose and meaning in their suffering. When the Jews were taken into captivity, God comforted them by assuring them that He had a plan and a purpose for them: "For I know the plans I have for you, says the Lord. They are plans for good and not for evil, to give you a future and a hope."[31]

When Answers Aren't Enough

For some of you reading this book, especially if you are going through suffering presently, these explanations of "purpose in suffering" seem totally inadequate. Though you may believe them to be true, they still ring hollow.

When my daughter was 18 months old, she needed her lip sewn; my explanations could not be appreciated or even understood. During our struggle with Susan's leukemia, I hurt so much and the probable outcome seemed so terrible that I did not even want to try and apply these principles for a number of months. Yet I was able to be thankful to God for who He was and I knew He cared even though I often did not *feel* like He cared. I also knew that ultimately these principles would be applicable to me.[32]

The following song rang true to me at a time when answers were not enough. During this time it was the assurance of God's love and ultimate resolution of my temporal problems that sustained me.

> When answers aren't enough, there is Jesus,
> He is more than just an answer to your prayer.
> And your heart will find a safe and peaceful
>   refuge,
> When answers aren't enough, He is there.[33]

–8–

Promises to Hold Onto

"Pssssss—tssss . . . pssssss—tssss." Hour after hour the respirator hissed on, "Pssssss—tssss. . . ." and Meryl Groce's life depended completely upon that machine. She lay in the intensive-care-unit bed totally alert with a clear mind, yet completely paralyzed except for the ability to move a couple of fingers. A few days earlier she had been in perfect health; now she lay stricken with an illness whose name she had never heard before: Guillain-Barre disease. The first three weeks, when she could barely communicate at all, were the worst, but it was during this period of time that she became acutely aware of God's presence. He seemed to be talking to her.

It was as if God wanted to get her attention. First, she felt Him assuring her, saying, "Don't be afraid. You're going through some rough times now, but I want to talk to you. You've had enough hurts in the past. You are going to be okay. I want you to trust Me." And so, somehow, Meryl did.

Then she became aware of one message, over and over again: "Meryl, I love you." Though Meryl was a typical churchgoer, she was not easily convinced that God loved her. So Meryl argued with God: "But I don't do what I'm supposed to. I don't read my Bible enough; I don't witness." And the voice came back to her again saying, "It's okay, Meryl—I love you. I understand."

Then she argued: "But I'm the girl that always was ripping the pocket off my dress—everything seemed to break as soon as I touched it. All my dolls had broken arms, and their heads were on sideways."

Then the anguish of the past started coming out. One of Meryl's children had been born with severe neurological and mental problems and finally had to be institutionalized. "Why, God—why?" she cried out. "Why did you let my son go through this pain?" And to all this outpouring God simply replied, "I love you and I love your son. You are very special to me."

Meryl was dependent on that respirator for more than two months and was hospitalized for almost three months. Except for a slight speech difficulty, Meryl recovered totally and returned to teaching. Now she is able to look back and say, "I can see that God really was guiding me all my life, even though there were times when I thought He didn't hear me or didn't understand. He was just waiting for His time to talk to me. God was very, very close during my illness. I felt His complete acceptance of me and I am singularly blessed in having had those weeks with the Lord."

Through this severe illness, Meryl gained an entirely new outlook upon life. She realizes that she is a special person whom God really loves despite her human frailties. She possesses a new sense of self-worth, a new sense of purpose and strength.

We humans would like God to be a genie, magically making every problem vanish from our lives, whether it be leukemia or lost keys. However, God does not guarantee that He will take away all our problems. What He does promise is to help us through them. The following are specific, unalterable principles or promises that He makes to us who desire to please Him—assurances to remember and cling to in times of pain.

Seven Assurances in Suffering

First of all, *we can be assured of God's phenomenal love and forgiveness.* As emphasized previously, much of our suffering is not due to our personal sin. However, even when it is the result of our personal sin, God assures us that He still loves us and is ready to forgive us. He is always desirous that we would come into a right relationship with Him through Christ. We are promised that "If we confess our sins, He is faithful and righteous to forgive us our sins and to cleanse us from all unrighteousness."[1] If this issue is not resolved in your mind, discuss it with a trusted friend, counselor, or pastor. You might find Billy Graham's book *Peace with God* very helpful at this time. See the application section for further direction.

Second, *God has allowed all the suffering we face.* He is sovereign and retains ultimate control of the universe. It has passed through the sieve of His permissive will. "But through it all, He would not allow one thing to be done apart from His decision."[2]

Third, *God will never give you more than you can bear.* God always sets limits on the amount of suffering or misfortune that occurs in your life. "No temptation [or suffering] has overtaken you but such as is common to man; and God is faithful, who will not allow you to be tempted [or suffer] beyond what you are able, but with the temptation [or suffering] will provide the way of escape also, that you may be able to endure it."[3]

Fourth, *often it is God's desire to deliver you from your current suffering.* "And Jesus was going about . . . healing every kind of disease and every kind of sickness. And seeing the multitudes, He felt compassion for them, for they were distressed and downcast like sheep without a shepherd."[4] More will be said about this in subsequent chapters.

God always cares and will go with us through the suffering is the fifth assurance. While God may not deliver you immediately from suffering, He is always very concerned about you when you are confronted with difficulty and will always go through it with you. Just because you feel He is distant does not mean that He is.

The Bible clearly states that God is aware of the minutest details of our lives—He even has numbered the hairs on our heads. If God cares enough to keep track of the hairs on your head, He certainly cares about whatever pain you may be having. "For God has said, 'I will never, never fail you nor forsake you.' That is why we can say without any doubt or fear, 'The Lord is my Helper and I am not afraid of anything that mere man can do to me.' "[5] One of the names of Christ is Immanuel which means "God with us." Though God may not *feel* close when your body is racked with suffering, the fact is that *God is with you.*[6]

Paul Lindell was dying of cancer when he wrote the following words: "I have read that a father whose son was killed in the Viet Nam War demanded to know, 'Where was God when my son was killed?' His old pastor answered kindly, 'Just where He was when His own Son was killed at Calvary.' "[7] Just as God was concerned about His Son, He is concerned about us, though it may not be perceived at the time of suffering.

Sixth, *God makes all things work together for ultimate good.* If we are yielded to Him, God can take the most adverse situation in our lives and ultimately use it for good. "And we know that God causes all things to work together for good to those who love God. . . ."[8]

Seventh, *God will more than make it up to you and will someday tell you why.* If in this life we are not delivered from our affliction, God will richly repay in heaven. He will be no man's debtor. God assures us that He will more than make it up to us in the end: "I know how much you suffer for the Lord, and I know all about your poverty (but you have heavenly riches!)."[9] And remember: The time of pain in this life is only an instant when compared to eternity.

You may not now understand the cause and purpose for your suffering, but God promises that someday you will understand. "Now all that I know is hazy and blurred, but then I will see everything clearly, just as . . . God sees. . . . "[10]

Many people find their greatest comfort in four words: *You are never alone*. In all of these promises we are assured, even when we do not feel like He is there, God will go through our suffering with us.

Once Susan was asked what questions needed answering in order to make it through her ordeal. She replied as follows:

"I am convinced that you don't have to have rational answers to the theological sticklers in order to make it through an ordeal like mine. It so happens that I did know 'the answers'—all the theory about why God allows suffering and how He uses it [that we talk about in this book]—but that's not what ultimately made the difference. What I had to do was be convinced that *God does care*. To do that I had to simply reiterate what I had learned in the past about God—from experience and from Scripture. I had to remember that Jesus always healed out of compassion (though there were often other reasons, too). I had to put aside my questions and fear and simply focus on God by reading psalms or listening to music. Though when I started doing these things I often didn't *feel* like God cared, by declaring His care to be a fact, the feelings did come.

"A song I frequently sang to remind myself of God's concern for me was one I learned as a short-term missionary in Guatemala the summer before developing leukemia. 'Diós está aquí . . .': 'God is here as certain as the air I breathe, as certain as the sun's rising in the morning. So certain that when I talk to Him, He is able to hear. God is here.'

"I affirmed a second belief that proved significant in getting through it all by reminding myself of the following: *God is in control* even if I have no clue why He's allowed all this; even though I am certain He has the power to heal me, and don't understand why He hasn't.

Everything I have is a gift—even my very life—even my birth in a country where I can get chemo—and God can do with it as He will. I'm a casualty in the celestial battle between God and all the evil in the world—including all the sin of the entire human race. But God will ultimately bring good out of it all. He is in control. This attitude is my definition of faith."

–9–

How God Heals

How Illness Develops

In the first part of this book, I discussed the theological origins of the problem of sin and sickness; in the last half I will focus on practical solutions to this problem. But before going on to the answers, let's take a brief look at the specifics of the problem: how illness develops in man.

Imagine that a group of skiers isolated in a remote Austrian lodge is exposed to infectious hepatitis. According to statistics, half of them would not be affected at all, and the other half would come down with hepatitis. Their symptoms would run the gamut from quite mild to extremely severe. The majority would recover completely; some would develop chronic hepatitis that would incapacitate them to various extents the rest of their lives; some would even die. Interestingly enough, if you tested the half that did not become ill, a significant number would have been infected with the virus, even though they never developed any symptoms. So, strictly speaking, they had hepatitis, too. Why are there such diverse outcomes? The reason is that there are a multitude of factors affecting any one outcome. Some skiers may have been exposed to a larger quantity of the virus in the first place; other skiers to almost none. Some strains of the virus may have been more aggressive than others. Then there are innumerable host factors—the overall condition of the person playing "host" to the virus. Some people may have developed an immunity to hepatitis from a previous exposure to the virus. Variations in a person's immune response, enzyme system, nutritional habits, and any current health problems will all affect the seriousness of the illness.[1]

Still, this illustration only offers an inkling of all the factors involved when a person contracts an illness, because so far we have only discussed the biological factors.

The mystery of the biological causes of illness began to be solved with Pasteur's discovery of the "pathogen" or germ; however, in the ensuing century, a host of other factors influencing the outcome of illness have been cataloged. Environmental studies have clarified the role of pollutants and carcinogens in illness. Genetic studies have unraveled the secrets of the genetic code and discovered that predispositions for certain illnesses tend to run in families.

But only more recently has the medical profession accepted the impact of emotional and even spiritual factors. For example, emotions, stress, and fatigue were found to affect significantly the healing of tuberculosis.[2] The eminent British physician, Sir William Osler, once noted: "The care of tuberculosis depends more on what the patient has in his head than what he has in his chest."[3]

The well-known "Social Readjustment Rating Scale," developed by Holmes and Rahe, assigns numerical values to stresses which greatly enhance the likelihood of developing an illness. If a person scores over 300 points, there is a 90-percent probability of his becoming ill within a year.[4] For years we have recognized the loss of a spouse as one of the most stressful occurrences of life; morbidity and mortality increase notably for up to ten years after the death of a spouse. The bereaved are three times more likely to die than those who have not been bereaved.[5]

The crucial question is exactly *how* does the mind affect the body? Are there any scientific explanations for this phenomenon? It has been shown in recent studies that the stressful experiences that impact one's health actually affect the central nervous system, thereby suppressing immune function. In particular, stress affects the portion of the brain called the hypothalamus, depressing the disease-fighting capability of both the overall body chemistry and the individual cells. A whole new area of medical knowledge is rapidly emerging called psychoneuroimmunology. The basic premise of this field is that our thoughts and feelings affect the nervous system, which then alters the immune response of our bodies.[6] Altered immune systems have been identified in individuals who are severely depressed, lonely, under stress, bereaved, separated, divorced, or undergoing significant marital conflict.

The magnitude and number of all these biological and emotional stresses will affect our bodies' internal responsiveness to disease, but they are by no means the final determinant. Equally important is our own response to the disease, the steps we take to prevent or alleviate it.[7] We have absolutely no control over some of the factors which cause disease; others, however, are partially or even totally under our control. By understanding this and developing a more complete perspective on illness, we can prevent or minimize disease in our lives.

The ordinary cold sore graphically illustrates the interaction of factors over which we have control and those over which we have no control. In individuals who are prone to these infections, the herpes simplex virus permanently resides in the tissue in the area where the infection habitually breaks out. The virus remains dormant when the person is in good health. But if he gets the flu, a cold, or a high fever, or becomes overtired, emotionally upset, or overstressed, the scales are tipped just enough to activate the virus, and a painful cold sore breaks out. Although this person has absolutely no control over the fact that he has the virus, he usually does have some control over things like getting run-down or letting himself be exposed to a cold or the flu.

In summation, if we seek to understand how illness develops, it will help us understand both our own role and God's role in the healing process.

God's Natural Healing

The flip side to how illness develops is how healing comes about. God has equipped our bodies with marvelous innate restorative powers. A small cut on the finger—which we erroneously call a "simple" cut—requires that a complex clotting system go into effect to prevent us from bleeding to death. A scab then forms, allowing the lacerated skin to be reunited and healed underneath. Because healing is a natural, everyday function of our bodies—like digesting food or pumping blood—keeping our bodies in basic good health is the first step in aiding the healing process. The clean-living person who exercises, eats right, and stays in shape "can expect to live eleven years longer than his sedentary, smoking, heavy-drinking counterpart."[8]

An old adage goes, "God heals, but the doctor collects the fees." In reality, this has a lot of truth to it. All of our medical and surgical skills merely serve to assist the natural healing processes with which our bodies come ready-equipped. The orthopedic surgeon may align two ends of a fractured bone, but if the body did not do its work of forming new bone, his efforts would be in vain. Even the most marvelous of the new advances in medicine are utterly dependent on one thing—the body's innate ability to heal itself. In the final analysis, medicine only serves to give the body an additional *healing edge*.

Is there, in the same manner, a mental-psychological and spiritual edge that we can identify and use to assist our bodies in their natural healing process? I think there is.

The powerful influence of our mind has been known for centuries. Solomon said about 3000 years ago, "A joyful heart is good medicine."[9] Galen, who lived in the second century, noted the relationship between cancer and depression. For centuries, people have walked on red-hot stones barefoot—without being burned. Childbirth, amputations of legs, and dental extractions have all been accomplished without the patient feeling any pain, because they were under hypnosis. Hypnotic suggestion has been used to decrease bleeding after surgical procedures and has made warts go away, which, incidentally, are virus-induced tumors. When participants in drug studies are given a placebo or "sugar pill" instead of the real medication, many have shown significant healing, simply because they believe it will heal them.

Though you may not personally want to walk on coals or be hypnotized, these all demonstrate the tremendous, God-given power that the mind has over healing our bodies.[10] Just as we must understand the principles of gravity, aerodynamics, and combustion in order to build an airplane that will transport us through the air, so the better we understand good health principles, the more we will be able to get a *healing edge* on sickness, thus assisting our bodies in the healing process.

Norman Cousins popularized this idea of assisting your body with the healing process in his book *Anatomy of an Illness*. In particular, he believed that laughter could help a person get well. He is convinced that a positive outlook, humor, and vitamins played a significant role in his recovery from an arthritic condition.[11]

Studies have shown that psychological treatment of patients with advanced cancer enabled the patients to live up to twice as long as those who did not have this treatment.[12]

As researchers have learned how to measure the immune function in the body, it has become clear that relaxation, good coping skills, social involvement, and good interpersonal relationships such as a good marriage enhance the immune system's ability to do such things as decrease complications in pregnancy and fight disease.[13] On the other hand, loneliness, stress, clinical depression, anxiety, divorce, and bereavement have all been shown to depress the immune system.[14]

In conclusion, it is my belief that as we understand and apply these principles, we will maximize the God-given capacity of our bodies both to prevent illness and to alleviate it, thus acquiring a *healing edge* in our lives.[15]

God's Miraculous Healing

After studying several prominent types of faith healers, Dr. William Nolen wrote a book titled *Healing: A Doctor in Search of a Miracle*. Although his study left him still searching for a miracle, he wrote: "I have become increasingly aware that all of healing is, in a very real sense of the word, miraculous. God has given us minds, the workings of which we have barely begun to comprehend, and using those minds, we have been able to find the answers to many of the puzzling disorders that afflict us."[16]

This author is not alone in his search for a miracle. The trouble is that many people are so eager to find one that they will call most anything a miracle. Speaking as a physician who has seen the word used very loosely, I feel we need to define the word before we go any further. To me, a strict definition of a miracle is an occurrence that either defies or supersedes all known and understood phenomena. Webster defines a miracle as "an extraordinary event manifesting divine intervention in human affairs." If asked, most physicians would agree with this definition, and it is the definition that I personally am most comfortable with. However, I find I fight an uphill battle if I try to persuade other people to hold to this strict definition. Many people use it to mean a marvelous, unlikely, phenomenal occurrence, as in this alternate meaning given by Webster: "An extremely outstanding or unusual event, or accomplishment."[17] The crucial difference is that in the strict definition, something must be supernatural to be a miracle; in the looser definition, it only need be unusual. Thus when the word "miraculous" is used, we must look at the supporting information to determine whether the incident is unequivocally supernatural.

Physicians are not only reluctant to call something miraculous, in an illness like cancer they are also loathe to use the word "cure." Cancer is often not cured, but instead goes into remission and then recurs. But what about the miraculous cures that doctors have reported—ones that cannot be explained by medical means and where the normal course of the illness would have resulted in death? The first such report appeared in a journal in 1897, documenting the mysterious disappearance of breast cancer that had previously spread throughout the body. In the decades since then, the scientific literature has been sprinkled with reports of cures or spontaneous regressions of cancer. In 1974, Dr. Warren H. Cole reported in an American Cancer Society journal that he and a colleague had found 176 cases that appeared in medical literature over the previous 70 years in which there was a confirmed diagnosis of cancer, and the regression could not be attributed to medical treatment. The researchers scrupulously excluded hundreds of other cases that did not meet their strict criteria and concluded that the phenomenon of medically unexplained cures is extremely rare—possibly "as low as one in 100,000 cancer patients." So while modern medicine cautions that this phenomenon is rare, it does admit that the phenomenon does in fact occur.[18]

In a follow-up study, Dr. Harvey W. Baker reported that between 1966 and 1985 at least 188 additional cases of cancer reported in the literature regressed spontaneously. He concluded, "It appears that almost every known type of malignant... neoplasm has regressed spontaneously." Baker's conclusions were far more optimistic than the conclusions of the prior study. He wrote: "While the spontaneous regression of cancer is a striking example of host control, it is a rare phenomenon, occurring in less than one in 1,000 cases. A far more common example, with which we are all familiar, is the prolonged survival of patients without therapy or with therapy known to be ineffective.... While spontenous regression is an admittedly rare occurrence, I believe the published reports may be only the tip of the iceberg."[19]

Dr. Charles Weinstock is even more optimistic. He says, "Until recently, the medical schools taught cancer as a one way process and rarely if ever mentioned either 'spontaneous' regressions or the host-resistance factor as a significant inter-individual variable (with particular reference to the cellular immune system)." He believes there are many more spontaneous regressions than are being reported. He also found out that such regressions usually came after some positive event in the person's life, such as a reconciliation, writing a book, the birth of a grandchild, a religious conversion, or intercessory prayer.[20]

Dr. Bernard Siegel, a surgeon who teaches at Yale University, has been encouraging patients to focus on what he calls the "exceptional," both in themselves and in the world around them. He says, "Since I've changed my approach to focus on these rarities... I hear about 'miraculous' healings everywhere I go."[21]

And so, even though loathe to admit it, the medical profession has been forced to agree that miracles do happen. What about the religious community's view on miracles? First of all, any truly biblically-based church has little choice but to believe in miracles. Even the most cursory look into the Scriptures provides ample evidence that our God is a God of miracles. And the miracles recorded in the Bible were not what you might call today's "easy miracles," like someone throwing away a crutch, or someone being "healed" from a disease whose natural course is to wax and wane, or someone whose illness has strong psychological aspects and thus the hope of a miracle in and of itself has a curative effect. The miracles of the Scriptures were atrophied arms made whole, individuals born blind given sight, the dead raised back to life—in other words, unequivocal miracles. I once heard a skeptic remark that he had seen piles of crutches left behind after a modern-day healing meeting, but he has never seen artificial legs left behind. However, we find in the Bible that Jesus was not limited to "easy miracles."[22]

So the question in religious circles usually is not "Does God do miracles?" We know from reading the Bible that He does. The more pressing questions are, "Does God do miracles as much *today* as He did in Bible times? Or does He do them at all today?" Most of us have come to believe that miracles were the norm in the Bible. But the Bible covers well over 2000 years of history, and miracles are not evenly distributed throughout those years. On the contrary, miracles cluster around pivotal events in the history of God's self-revelation to man. Furthermore, these miracles took place among a select group of people and in a very limited geographic area. Jesus did not heal in Greece or India or China. When He visited the pool of Bethesda, by which all of Jerusalem's diseased and crippled would come to sit because of its healing waters, He restored to health only one man. Why not all of them? Some people might answer that just one man had the faith; the Bible says in many places that Jesus could not heal certain people because they lacked faith. However, the man at the pool of Bethesda made no request of Jesus—he did not even know who Christ was. All he did was grumble to Jesus about having no one to help him into the pool when the angel touched its waters—only the first person in would be healed. In my opinion, Jesus chose to heal that particular man not because he deserved it or exhibited any spectacular faith but to demonstrate God's power.[23]

Jesus' purposes for coming to earth were not to heal all the sick and feed all the hungry, although He healed and fed many. He lived among men so He could manifest God's character, verify the fact of His deity, and pay the price for our sin through His death and resurrection. God's ultimate purpose was achieved: to make it possible for every person to have a personal relationship with Him.

Christ's miracles served primarily as signs; they verified His claim of being God. "Believe me when I say that I am . . . [God]; or at least believe on the evidence of the miracles themselves."[24] Before Jesus restored a paralytic, He told the critics who were watching Him that He was going to heal the man "in order that you may know that the Son of Man has authority on earth to forgive sins," which was an obvious claim to divinity.[25] Likewise, at the time of Moses, God sent plagues "that will really speak to you and to your servants and to all the Egyptian people, and prove to you there is no other God in all the earth."[26] The miracles recorded in Acts served in part to authenticate the Holy Spirit's presence with the fledgling church. So to summarize: This function of miracles was to verify God's new and unprecedented presence among a group of people at critical points in the history of Israel and the church.

A common problem in religious circles today is that it is exceedingly easy to overemphasize the whole area of miraculous healing, allowing it to eclipse the entire gospel message, and to seek such manifestations of God's power for the wrong reasons. Christ Himself warned against such motives.[27]

David Watson, an Anglican minister, describes his struggle with cancer in his excellent book *Fear No Evil*:

> Over the years I have seen a number of faith-healers at work, and most have left me troubled, if not disillusioned. The strong emotionalism of the meeting, the persuasive pleas for money, the unconfirmed claims of healing—all have left me wary and skeptical. . . . Over the years I have been confused and cautious about the whole subject. I have not doubted that God *can* heal, and I have sometimes experienced heal-ing myself, but it has very much been the exception rather than the rule.[28]

Jesus made the place and purpose for miracles very clear to His disciples. He told the disciples when they were jubilant after healing people and casting out de-mons, "Do not rejoice in this, that the spirits are subject to you, but rejoice that your names are recorded in heaven."[29] God gives us evidence of His power to en-courage our faith, but He does not want our faith to *depend* upon seeing miracles. Christ did not refuse Thomas' de-mand to touch His miraculously healed wounds, but He admonished him, "Because you have seen Me, have you believed? Blessed are they who did not see, and yet believed."[30]

It is my opinion that God considers seeking the mirac-ulous alone, and merely for its own sake, a perversion. I believe God is more apt to bless those who trust Him without *demanding* to see supernatural events. For those people, He may more readily choose to intervene mirac-ulously in their lives.

My Personal Perspective on Miracles

As a physician who is a Christian, I frequently read and hear about miraculous healings. To be candid, most of these can be explained if you know the natural course of the illness—the ups and downs, the ebb and flow—and the effects of the medical treatment the person is having. On the other hand, I have seen some phenomenal healings that came very close to, if not in fact were, miraculous. I know of a pastor whose chest X-ray showed a large mass in the lung. His physician concluded from the X-rays and the lab tests that it was cancer. After prayer, all the surgeon could find when he operated was a blob of necrotic (dead) tissue. My father had urinary bleeding a number of years ago, and an X-ray revealed what the radiologist said was unequivocally cancer of the kidney. However, surgery revealed only a benign cyst. And now, Susan's deliverance after such a close brush with death is phenomenal. To me, healings like this that I have witnessed certainly are strongly suggestive of God's intervention.

I fully believe that God performs miracles today—to believe less is to limit God. On the other hand, it is my opinion that miraculous healing, using the strict definition, is not as widespread today as some claim it to be.

However, medical explanations for cures need not detract from God's glory. God often works behind the scenes in "logical" means. Someone then can choose to focus on the logic or to see God's providential hand. For example, there was a passenger who was scheduled to fly on American Airlines flight #191 from Chicago to Los Angeles. He had to deal with the frustration of a canceled connecting flight only to find out later that #191 had crashed, killing all on board. He believes God was working behind the scenes preventing his death.[31] It has been said that "coincidence is God's way of remaining anonymous."[32]

The Pharisees who witnessed Jesus' miracles attributed His power to Satan, whereas today's agnostic cites medical technicalities and minute statistical probabilities.[33] Either way, a person chooses what he will believe and to whom or to what he will give glory: to man, to the "miracle" of modern medicine, to whatever supernatural forces or philosophy he happens to believe in—or to God. I give God the glory for healings that come through both natural and miraculous means. "Every good and perfect gift is from above, coming down from the Father." I would add that all wisdom, health, and healing come to us from God also.[34]

Part IV
Finding Meaning in Suffering

–10–

Face Your Feelings

We had just taken Susan in for her first hospitalization at U.C.L.A. and were still reeling from the impact of the diagnosis. After she got situated in her isolation room, Betty and I walked to a restaurant close to the campus to get a bite to eat. On our way we passed clusters of U.C.L.A. students frolicking around. All of a sudden anger surged through me. "It's not fair that all these college students are so carefree while my daughter is in the hospital with leukemia and only a 10- to 15-percent possibility of being alive in five years!"

The next Sunday evening I was sitting in church listening to some young people happily singing Christian songs, and again it made me angry. When church was over, I snuck out as quickly as possible, not wanting to talk to a soul, agitated by the question, "Why is this happening to us?"

Down deep inside I realized the issue wasn't really "Why is this happening to us?" but "I don't like what is happening to us—it's not fair." I understood many of the whys of suffering; after all, I had already written much of this manuscript. But frankly, I just did not like what was happening. It seemed that so many of our dreams were being dashed to pieces.

I have heard a story about an experiment a man tried: He decided to go up and down a particular street in a neighborhood and give the occupant of each home a $100 bill every day for a month. On the first day of his experiment he went to each house, and the residents questioned his motives. They would hesitantly take the money, all the while wondering what the gimmick was.

After several days, however, when the people had spent the money and had proven that it was genuine, the entire neighborhood buzzed with excitement over these daily gifts. By the second week, the residents were waiting for the stranger and his money. By the third week, people from neighboring streets were loitering about to witness this event. Then, on the last day of the month, the man merely walked slowly down the street but did not give out any money. The residents became irate, shouting angrily at him, "Where's my $100 bill?"

What had happened? Something that started out as a gift was taken for granted when it was given on a regular basis. They perceived it as something that was owed to them, and when they stopped getting it they became angry. Isn't that what we often find ourselves doing? God gives us so many wonderful things, and before long they become expected. When we lose these perceived "rights" we grow angry at God, at others, or at life itself. God had given my wife and me a wonderful daughter and we always just assumed she would live a long, healthy life. So when her very life was threatened, it aroused overwhelming feelings in us—feelings that typically accompany suffering.

Strong Feelings Typically Accompany Suffering

Strong emotions normally accompany a tragedy or crisis. So the first step in healing is to honestly face those negative feelings, uncomfortable as they may be. We do not need to look far in the Scriptures to find people who allowed themselves to express their feelings. Paul expressed his confusion by questioning: "We are afflicted in every way, but not crushed; perplexed, but not despairing."[2] David poured out his complaint: "Day and night I weep. . . . O my soul, why be so gloomy and discouraged?"[3] Yet religious leaders often do a great injustice by denying people who are suffering the right to feel strong negative emotions.

Even medical research shows the importance of not denying our feelings. Individuals who express their feelings actually live longer than those who do not. In a study of victims with breast cancer, those who "... were communicative about their distress... [and] appeared more capable of externalizing their negative feelings ... survived longer."[4] Another study found a strong correlation between helpless stoic acceptance and a poorer prognosis.[5]

Many of these noncommunicative individuals may not be aware of a number of common emotional phases that sufferers go through. People stricken by any kind of crisis typically experience a number of negative phases. It has been widely accepted that there are five stages that people tend to go through when confronted with a life-threatening illness. Those stages are denial and isolation, anger, bargaining, depression, and acceptance.[6] I would add several other significant feelings that most people face: anxiety and uncertainty, guilt, and anger at or distance from God.

A common reaction to a life-threatening illness is to deny that it even exists. Men with severe chest pain may say, "It's only heartburn." A woman who notices a lump in her breast often denies for months that it could be serious before seeking medical help.

Denial can be defined as a conscious or unconscious defense mechanism, used to repudiate the meaning of an event or to allay fear, anxiety, or other unpleasant emotions. For instance, Susan experienced a degree of denial periodically throughout her illness as when she recorded in her journal while hospitalized: "I am going to put on clothes this evening, that will feel better—I'M NOT SICK!!!"

For some Christians, however, this denial takes on a "spiritual" guise as they express their conviction of a miraculous healing despite the progression of their symptoms. It is my opinion that this kind of denial does not bring honor to God and, unfortunately, keeps many from seeking the medical care they need.

The phase that often follows denial is anger, an emotion that frequently erupts when we face difficulties. Susan recorded her strong feelings of anger:

> It's one month since the start of chemo and I've been mad: Mad at the doctors who said I might "bounce back" quicker this time. Yeah— *Might*. Mad at myself for hoping I might. Really specifically mad at myself for hoping I'd get out yesterday or today (of isolation, that is). Hearing my counts yesterday I figured I would not make it today, either. Guess what, I was right. What's more, the differential went *down*! Of all the nerve!
>
> Oh, I need to laugh at myself. But I'm hanging on to this bad mood. I was snappy with Mom and Mrs. Speight, yet they weren't ruffled. I hate the nurses (not really, but I feel like it); their very presence rubs in my position. I want privacy, *no drugs*, decent food, no masks! I keep having to stop writing 'cause I start crying. I try not to let myself cry—it's like I'd rather be mad. But actually, the tears are probably a good release.

Five months later, after her relapse, Susan's angry feelings were often aroused by upbeat Christian songs telling about how wonderful it is to be a Christian: "They made me angry because things sure weren't wonderful for me and I knew that all my life my highest priority had been to know, love, and serve God."

I have had to struggle with my own feelings of anger that crop up when I am tempted to think about how unfair I feel Susan's illness is. Many Christians tend to look at anger as wrong and thus are prone to bury it. However, we find biblical heroes such as David, Job, Elijah, and Habakkuk all getting angry at God or declaring to God their anger at an unjust situation.

One recent study revealed that if a person buries anger that he has a valid reason to express, it can actually increase the likelihood that the person will die earlier: "Persons who would hold in their anger to their spouse were 2.4 times as likely to die over the [12-year] follow-up period compared with those who would express their anger to their mate." In fact this is a higher risk to the individuals than high blood pressure, decreased lung capacity, excessive weight, cigarette smoking, etc. Individuals with elevated blood pressure who also scored high on the suppressed anger index were five times as likely to have died during the follow-up period.[7]

It is my opinion that anger, in and of itself, is not wrong unless it is about the wrong thing, misused, or we get stuck in this phase.[8]

Guilt is another common emotion that torments us in times of suffering. So often we are besieged by the "what if's." "What if I had gone to the doctor sooner?" "What if I had followed a healthier diet?" "What if I had had my brakes checked?" Or even, "What if I had lived a life more devoted to God?" Sometimes it's even our closest friends who raise the questions that make us feel guilty. Hopefully, in all these situations we can differentiate between specific, actual reasons for guilt and vague, gnawing guilt feelings. Then we can deal with the treatable issues and put the false guilt aside.[9]

Another source of guilt for those stricken with illness is questions about whether their thoughts or mental attitudes have played a role. Susan remembers that as a teenager she sometimes had dramatic heroine daydreams of being stricken with some illness or tragedy.

When she was first in the hospital she had to remind herself that such fantasies are common among adolescent girls and were not the self-induced cause of her leukemia. She also wrestled with the self-doubt of, "Does some part of me really want to be sick?" For some people this is certainly a valid question, but in Susan's situation it wasn't true.

Anxiety and uncertainty also accompany severe illnesses. Many Christians would consider these feelings wrong, quoting the verse, "Be anxious for nothing."[10] However, a number of other verses tell us that strong leaders throughout the Scriptures had their times of anxiety. Paul wrote about his "constant worry of how the churches are getting along," and Jesus Himself was "deeply troubled" during His suffering.[11]

Depression is another exceedingly common reaction to suffering. The loss of anything important to us will normally result in depression. Again, many individuals in the Scriptures such as Elijah, David, and Job suffered from depression.[12]

The cumulative effects of negative emotions such as anger, false guilt, and depression, as well as the physical effects of the illness itself, all tend to make us *feel* that God is very distant. While suffering with cancer, David Watson said:

> Although I proclaim that God is real and answers prayer, to be honest he sometimes seems a million miles away and strangely silent to my frightened cries. But I have discovered over the years that although God never promises to save us from suffering, he does promise to be with us in the midst of it and is himself afflicted by it.
>
> The mystics down the centuries have often referred to "the dark night of the soul." This

describes those periods when God seems strangely silent and absent in spite of personal need. We wonder what he is doing, why he is withholding his presence from us. We pray to him, but the heavens seem as brass and we feel trapped by the prison of our own dark moods. "The greatest test of a Christian's life is to live with the silence of God" wrote Bishop Mervyn Stockwood in a letter to me recently. How far can we go on trusting God when we have no experience of his love? Is it enough to take him purely at his word when we feel no reality behind those familiar phrases?[13]

Susan tells of her own struggles with her feelings:

"After my relapse I was troubled by the 'claim it in faith' theologies that had been presented to me. While I was still able to read, I studied the gospels to see what they said or inferred about faith. One day I read the story of Jesus calming the sea and then rebuking the disciples for their lack of faith. I related to the disciples. They were simply and naturally afraid for their lives; those emotions often can't be helped no matter what you know. *It said that Jesus was grieved with them, and that hurt me terribly—was Christ grieved and even angry with me for my lack of faith—because I was afraid?* I wasn't afraid of dying per se. But I was terribly afraid of spending the rest of my life—a life of five years or less—constantly in and out of the hospital, on chemotherapy, fighting infections, and weak from vomiting and anemia. I was afraid of how much more pain I might have—and the uncertainty of it all. *That fear that God was displeased with my fear disturbed me off and on through most of that month.*

"I don't know if I ever fully resolved that question of whether or not my fear was a lack of faith. I did pray for forgiveness though, telling God that only He knew exactly how I felt and that I needed *Him* to give me the necessary faith—'Lord, I believe, help my unbelief.' I was fortunate in that, by faith, I knew God was with me, although I sometimes didn't *feel* His presence. My most common feeling was that God was standing nearby, but He wasn't telling me *anything* about what the future held for me."

The kinds of feelings Susan describes have been felt by countless people. Moreover, they often say that they find it difficult and even impossible to pray or read the Scriptures. Don't be surprised by such feelings but realize that their presence does not in itself constitute sin. The apostle Paul felt loneliness, disappointment, despair, and lack of support. David, a man after God's own heart, frequently hurled his questions at God: "Why, O Lord, do you stand far off? Why do you hide yourself in times of trouble?" And even the Son of God, while going through His agony on the cross, cried out, "My God, My God, why hast Thou forsaken Me?"[14]

Avoid Getting Stuck

It is crucial that we allow ourselves to get in touch with our negative feelings when calamity strikes; to do so actually helps us to deal with the situation better. On the other hand, "getting in touch with our feelings" is by no means synonymous with stewing in our own juices and becoming bitter for months, years, or even the rest of our lives. I have seen people stuck in bitterness from a divorce, loss of a job, or the death of a loved one, to name just a few examples. One such patient made the following comments to me: "I won't let anyone take the rage away from me. . . . I feel I have taken the wrong road—the road of vengeance and hate, I feel meaner and meaner. . . . I won't stop being angry. . . . The hate I have inside eats me up." As one might have predicted, this patient struggles with chronic depression.

This patient is an extreme example of one stuck in self-pity. Thomas Hermiz warns us: "You cannot give in to self-pity. The moment you wallow in self-pity, you are on dangerous ground and thin ice . . . [which] will turn into resentment."[15] Thielicke warns us: "The more I become immersed in myself, the more wretched I become. This wretchedness can lead to real sickness."[16] Robert Veninga, who studied numerous survivors of calamities, states, "The first, and perhaps most striking, characteristic of families who survive a tragedy is that they simply refuse to be bitter."[17]

You Have a Choice

The Chinese character for "crisis" is a combination of two other characters: "danger" and "opportunity." Moreover, an ancient Chinese definition of crisis is "opportunity riding on dangerous winds."

When faced with suffering we can regress emotionally, wallowing in bitterness and resentment, and waste the opportunity that the crisis affords. On the other hand, we can choose to discover the inherent opportunity in the situation amidst the pain, and thus make the most of the experience. John White writes in his book *The Fight*, "Tough times . . . do one of two things to you. They either break or make you. If you are not utterly crushed by them . . . you will be enlarged by them. Their pain will make you live more deeply and expand your consciousness. . . . "[18]

The Greek philosopher Plutarch said, "The measure of a man is the way he bears up under misfortune."[19] Another Greek, Epictetus—not a philosopher, but a Roman slave—said, "Men are disturbed not by things, but by the view they take of them." A modern writer puts it this way: "The calibre of a man is found in his ability to meet disappointment successfully, enriched rather then narrowed by it."[20]

In fact, medical studies have recently backed up these philosophers with evidence that it is not just the stresses in our lives that determine our emotional and physical states, but it is the way we perceive these stresses that affects our feelings and even our bodies' immune responses.[21]

Dr. Viktor Frankl, a Jewish psychiatrist, also affirms our personal freedom and responsibility to choose our responses. In *Man's Search for Meaning* he describes his harrowing years in Nazi prison camps:

> The experiences of camp life show that man does have a choice of action. There were enough examples, often of a heroic nature, which proved that apathy could be overcome, irritability suppressed. Man *can* preserve a vestige of spiritual freedom, of independence of mind, even in such terrible conditions of psychic and physical stress . . . everything can be taken from man but one thing: the last of human freedoms—to choose one's attitude in any given set of circumstances, to choose one's own way.
>
> And there were always choices to make. Every day, every hour, offered the opportunity to make a decision. . . .
>
> In the final analysis it becomes clear that the sort of person the prisoner became was the result of an inner decision, and not the result of camp influences alone. Fundamentally, therefore any man can, even under such circumstances, decide what shall become of him—mentally and spiritually.
>
> Whenever one is confronted with an inescapable, unavoidable situation . . . [such as] an incurable disease . . . , just then is one given a

last chance to actualize the highest value, to fulfil the deepest meaning, the meaning of suffering.

In the concentration camps, for example, in this living laboratory and on this testing ground, we watched and witnessed some of our comrades behave like swine while others behaved like saints. Man has both potentialities within himself; which one is actualized depends on decisions but not on conditions.[22]

I believe this is what Scripture means when it says, "All discipline for the moment seems not to be joyful, but sorrowful; yet to those who have been trained by it, afterwards it yields the peaceful fruit of righteousness."[23] The Phillips translation stipulates that the suffering must be "accepted in the right spirit. . . . " In his book *Fear No Evil*, David Watson gives yet another vivid example of the choices we have:

Two fathers came to me within a space of a few months. Each had lost a young child tragically. One child, aged four, had died of leukemia; the other, aged five, had drowned in a swimming pool in their own back garden. One father had been a professing Christian before the disaster but became a bitter and militant atheist as a result; the other had been a professing humanist but became a committed Christian as a result. They both had roughly the same suffering to contend with, but their reactions were widely different. One had his bitterness to endure as well as his suffering, which in the long run might well have been worse—it was certainly worse for other people; the other found the peace and love of Christ, which transformed his suffering. In all our

afflictions it is not so much our situation that
counts but the way in which we react to it. And
our reactions can affect, to a remarkable degree, the outcome of our lives.[24]

It is appropriate to conclude that "affliction may teach
us to pray" or it may "teach us to curse."[25]

–11–

Seek Appropriate Help

Seek God's Deliverance

It was a dreary Tuesday morning, January 31, 1984, and our emotions were tangled with fear and uncertainty as several of our church leaders and pastors arrived at our home. They greeted us warmly but their mood was serious. As their church chairman, I had worked closely with all these individuals for a number of years. If the situation had been different, they might have been coming lightheartedly and laughing—but not this morning. The previous afternoon Susan had been told she had leukemia. We had asked these leaders to come in accordance with the Scriptures to pray for her healing and anoint her with oil.[1] Some prayed for an immediate cure so that medical treatment would not be necessary. Others prayed that God would use the medical means as an avenue for healing. After a time of prayer and singing, they left, and Betty and I took Susan for her first hospitalization.

So it was on a number of occasions throughout 1984 and 1985 that we asked the church leaders to pray for Susan's healing. In addition, numerous people across the nation were praying for our family. Some people recommended that we take her to healing meetings, but we really did not feel that God was directing us to do that. Other people advised us to act on faith and take her out of the hospital even though her blood counts were so low that she could die without antibiotics, red cell, and platelet transfusions. I believe that if God had wanted us to take her out of the hospital, He would have restored her counts to normal, and then, to the amazement of the doctors, we could have had her discharged appropriately. I believe this course of action would have been consistent with Christ's instructions to those He healed of leprosy. He told them to be inspected by the priests and be given a clean bill of health before going back into society, from which they had been isolated.[2] The Parkers, referred to earlier, learned this lesson the hard way. They believed God would heal their diabetic son if they acted on faith and discontinued his insulin shots, only to have him die. In their book several years later they wrote: "Any genuine faith healing can stand the test of medical verification."[3]

During Susan's painfully slow recovery from the transplant, we all wondered at times if the graft would take. Since it would mean certain death if it did not, we as a family searched our hearts to see if there was anything else that we should do to seek God's intervention. We were willing to do anything that we felt God wanted us to do. The only additional act that we felt might be valid was to ask someone who believed he had the special gift of healing to pray for Susan. This we did.[4]

In all honesty, there were times that we prayed when it seemed like God's answer was either "no" or "wait." For instance, when she was in her first remission we asked that she would not have a recurrence. When she had the persistent high fevers and vomiting, we appealed for relief. But the answer was "no"—she did have a recurrence and there was little, if any, relief from the fevers and vomiting. On the other hand, there were numerous other times when the answer was "yes"— such as when her counts were down or when we were told that a bone marrow transplant was impossible— and God dramatically intervened.

Apropos to God's deliverance is the Old Testament account in the Book of Daniel of Shadrach, Meshach, and Abednego. King Nebuchadnezzar decided to cast them alive into a furnace of fire. They responded, "If it be so, our God whom we serve is able to deliver us from the furnace of blazing fire; and He will deliver us out of your hand, O king. But even if He does not, let it be known to you, O king, that we are not going to serve your gods."[5] They were convinced of God's sovereign power and ability to deliver miraculously. They believed that God would, in fact, deliver them, but they did not take away His sovereignty by telling God how He must handle the situation. So we also believed that God was able to supernaturally intervene and deliver Susan. However, we were aware that healing, ultimately, is always His choice and that we would continue to serve Him regardless of His choice.

Seek Medical Help

Over a month before that dismal Tuesday morning, Susan had a routine medical exam for what we thought were some minor physical symptoms. The lab work revealed a low white blood count, which to me suggested a serious illness, so within 24 hours we sought consultation from a specialist.

Quite obviously, I believe in seeking medical help. Some Christians, including friends of mine, question the use of medical help. I must differ with them on this point. I believe it is consistent with the Scriptures to seek medical help as long as we are aware that God alone is ultimately the source of all healing. Many people think that the Scripture's injunction to anoint the sick with oil is symbolic of asking God to anoint them with His Spirit.[6] On the other hand, some feel that this passage is speaking of giving medical help to the person, since putting oil on wounds was one of the common medical treatments of the day. We find a good example in the account of the Good Samaritan, who put oil on the man he found injured by the side of the road. When Jesus applied mud to the blind man's eyes, as recorded in the Gospel of John, He was following another common practice of the day; in addition, He gave His divine blessing and miraculous results followed. God instructed Hezekiah's servant to "prepare a poultice of figs and apply it to the boil and he will recover"—again a common treatment of that time. Likewise, Paul advised Timothy to employ the usual medicinal means of treating his stomach ailment.

An unfortunate phenomenon is that many people who have symptoms indicating a serious illness delay seeking help. This is especially true of those with cancer and heart disease. One study of individuals with symptoms that suggested cancer revealed that 66 percent waited longer than one month before seeking medical attention, 39 percent waited longer than three months, and 25 percent waited longer than six months. For some people the delay cost them their lives.[8]

My advice as a physician is to seek the best medical help available. In many instances this can be obtained in your community, but in certain situations, such as in Susan's, a more specialized medical center is crucial.

Seek out as much information about your illness as you are comfortable with and is necessary to assure that you obtain the proper treatment. However, beyond that it is a highly individual matter. Persons who are inquisitive generally do better when they are fully informed about their illness. On the other hand, those who do not want much information do worse if it is forced upon them, provided this does not keep them from seeking the necessary medical treatment.[9]

Speaking again as a physician, I encourage you to cooperate with your doctor. However, since Susan's illness I have learned that this advice needs to be qualifiea. A study revealed that patients who were polite, apologetic, almost painfully acquiescent to all doctors' recommendations experienced a more rapid progression of the disease, as contrasted with patients who were much more vocal and self-expressive.[10]

Since Susan has no biological siblings, we were told from the onset of her illness that a transplant was impossible, but a physician friend encouraged me to consider one. With the recurrence there was no medical possibility of a cure so I studied the literature on parent-child transplants and found that some medical centers were doing them. Then I called the chief of one of these centers who strongly encouraged me to pursue the possibility of a parent-child transplant.

With this encouragement I pressed the issue with her doctor: "Is there *any* chance of a parent-child match?"

"No, none. Ah, ah, well, theoretically there's a possibility," he said.

"Then let's try it," I pursued.

"But the tissue typing costs four hundred dollars apiece," he retorted.

I responded: "That's nothing compared to the tens of thousands of dollars that her medical expenses have run thus far."

Reluctantly he agreed to the typing. To his amazement, my tissue matched Susan's almost perfectly—a 1:5000 possibility! If I had not pushed Susan's physician against his advice to test for the possibility of a bone marrow transplant, it is almost certain that she would now be dead.

Dr. Bernie S. Siegel wrote the following in his book *Love, Medicine and Miracles*:

> Exceptional patients . . . take charge of their lives even if they were never able to before. . . . They do not rely on doctors to take the initiative but rather use them as members of a team demanding the utmost in technique,

resourcefulness, concern, and open-mindedness. If they're not satisfied, they change doctors. . . .

Participation in the decision-making process, more than any other factor, determines the quality of the doctor-patient relationship. The exceptional patient wants to share responsibility for life and treatment, and doctors who encourage that attitude can help all their patients heal faster.[11]

Use All the Available Resources

In addition to seeking God's supernatural intervention and appropriate medical treatment, Susan worked hard at having a good mental outlook, drawing on both spiritual as well as psychological principles. The following chapters will elaborate on these principles in detail.

In conclusion, Susan's healing exemplifies the cooperation of spiritual, medical, and psychological means of healing. Although doctors have not pronounced her cured, she has been completely free of leukemia for 44 months (as of the time of this writing) when she normally would have had a relapse in less than five months.

-12-

The Will to Health

"When I [Susan] was asked which were the most emotionally wearing aspects of my hospitalizations, I replied that foremost was the fear I felt when I knew I had relapsed. Second was the loss of control over my surroundings, daily activities, physical body, and emotions.

"That loss of control was most vividly experienced as reactions to some of the medications. Some of the antinausea drugs caused intense nervousness. I could not sit still for 30 seconds; I couldn't concentrate on even a simple conversation. Every second was an agony from which I couldn't be distracted. I paced up and down the hall and told every nurse and doctor that they had to take me off this; I would rather be vomiting. Another antinausea drug caused my muscles to contract. It nearly paralyzed me; every muscle was flexed, even my tongue —I couldn't talk. That was frightening—terrifying— and the fear made me even more tense.

"In addition to such dramatic examples, every area of my life was affected to some extent by this loss of control. Let me describe a typical morning out of my eight months in the hospital:

6:30 A.M. A technician wakes me up to draw blood.

7:40 A.M. The day nurse checks in on me.

8:10 A.M. My intern comes by for rounds, pokes me a little, and listens to my lungs with his cold stethoscope.

8:30 A.M.   Breakfast is brought in and the egg is cold. Yuk! Anyway I'm not hungry.

10:00 A.M. I take a sponge bath while a nurse makes my bed for me. I dress in a generic hospital gown that leaves as much exposed as it covers.

10:35 A.M. The nurse comes back to dress my wound, change my dressing, and clean the Hickman catheter which is permanently implanted in my chest.

10:50 A.M. I have just gotten settled down to try and concentrate on a TV show when the housekeeper and janitor troop in to clean the floor and empty the wastebaskets. Later, I am distracted as I notice that everyone's messed up *my room*! The technician left a tourniquet and bloody cotton ball on the table just out of my reach. The nurse left some gauze pads and a roll of tape on top of my books instead of in the box where they belong. The janitor rearranged my furniture so I can't even reach a Kleenex to blow my nose!

11:15 A.M. IV chemotherapy starts. It's supposed to help me, but as far as I can tell it just makes me shake with chills, nauseates me, and makes me irritable.

"Can you sense how the loss of control was so emotionally wearing? I found that this loss tended to result in boredom and depression which paralyzed my ability to make decisions and to take an interest in anything. After spending weeks in isolation, nothing anyone suggested to me sounded the least bit interesting or feasible. I could not concentrate enough to read; my hand shook too much to write; I don't like needlework; drawing seemed 'dumb.' I don't like crossword or jigsaw puzzles; TV's boring; and on it went! If you can't do the things you would really like to do, such as walking on the beach, it's hard to muster up any interest in activities that seem 'artificial.'

"I soon realized, though, that if I was physically and mentally incapable of doing the things I wanted to do, I needed to give up my demand to do those things and find some alternate activities. Not only did I need these activities to keep me occupied, but having specific tasks to accomplish gave me a measure of control over myself and my environment. Throughout the course of my illness, I learned more and more how to recognize the oft-taken-for-granted choices that I still had available to me, and how to gain control by exercising those choices.

"At first it was very difficult to see what things I had control over when trying to fend off boredom in the hospital. When I was unable to read—something I normally enjoy—I was tempted to just be irritated. Yet I knew I had to do something, so I finally allowed a friend to bring up a 'Doodle Art' poster and colored pens. I can't honestly say I enjoyed it—I felt rather childish having to work so hard to stay in the lines. But it certainly wasn't as bad as I expected, and it did fill a lot of empty time. Later, my mom brought up a simple latch-hook rug kit and, to my surprise, it turned out to be the perfect activity for that particular period of my illness! I found that in order to break out of the boredom, I had to force myself to do *something*—anything—even if my efforts were only halfhearted at first.

There Were Choices Available to Me

"At the beginning of each day I made it a habit to choose something I wanted to accomplish that day: clip my fingernails, write one thank-you note, call a friend,

visit another patient. In addition, my nurses told me
that the patients who make an effort to eat invariably do
better than those who don't even try; therefore, I decided that if I had to eat hospital food, at least *I* would
choose which dishes to order and try to eat at least a few
bites! I planned my days by reading the TV guide and
deciding which programs I would watch between other
activities or naps. I found it rewarding, though tiring,
just throwing out bits of trash, dusting the small ledge
by the window, or rearranging cards. I tried to keep
physically active: I would do stretching exercises on the
bed, walk in place, ride an exercycle, or shoot baskets
with a nerf ball. When I accomplished any task or made a
decision, no matter how small, I tried to congratulate
myself. This seemed to increase my self-confidence and
strengthen the feeling that I had *some* control over my
life.

   "Occasionally, a choice available to me seemed out-
landish or required the help of friends. For example,
during my second hospitalization I was complaining to
Linda Hibst that my room didn't have a bath! Sponge
baths get awfully old . . . how wonderful it would be to
be able to get into the water. Linda pondered the problem, then queried, 'Why couldn't you have a plastic
wading pool in here?' I was skeptical, but couldn't think
of any reason why not. So my daring friends bought a
child's wading pool, snuck it in the back door of the
hospital and up four flights of stairs. The next day I set it
in the middle of the floor, pulled the curtain, taped a 'Do
Not Disturb!' sign on the door, and filled it with a few
inches of warm water. Then—luxury—I sat cross-legged
in the water and watched TV while splashing it over me
until it got cold! Eventually, the nurses all came and
peeked, and didn't even mind helping me empty the
water and wipe up the splashes with the dirty towels.
With creativity and daring and helpful friends, many
problems can be solved.

"Despite such wonderful friends, many days there were just too many people intruding on me. I couldn't do anything about the various hospital personnel trooping in and out all day long, but I was able to have my parents screen visitors to some extent, which helped. Or, if people would call when I was feeling particularly bad, I learned not to feel guilty about saying, 'Thanks for calling, but I'm having a bad day. Would you mind calling another day when I'm feeling better?'

"Nevertheless, I couldn't always make myself eat, sound cheerful, or keep myself occupied. Sometimes I felt paralyzed with fear, helplessness, and lethargy, or lonely, bored, frustrated, angry—totally out of control of my life. Sometimes I gave in to these feelings; I snapped at nurses, treated visitors rudely, complained, and whined. But after such an episode I would confess my inappropriate and unpleasant behavior to God, write in my journal, or talk it over with John or my parents. Over and over again I found I had to keep trying to regain some measure of constructive control over myself and my emotions. It was work to apply the principles that would speed my recovery.

"Sometimes I had absolutely no control over my physical situation, such as when I lay shivering for days on an ice blanket with a 105-degree fever. Still, I found I could choose whether to hold on to my frustration or let go of it. I found that regardless of the circumstances I still had choices regarding my attitude. Even on bad days, when I wasn't sure what God was doing, when the doctors were not sure what was causing the high fevers, and I wasn't sure if visitors were a blessing or a curse—still I found that I had some choices. When I exercised my ability to choose, I found that the day went just a little bit better, at a time when it seemed as though everything was crashing around me."

The Need for Control Verified

What Susan learned about the need for control when she was in the hospital has been overwhelmingly verified in the medical literature. Dr. Eric Cassell, an internist at Cornell University Medical College, wrote in *The Healer's Art*, "If I had to pick the aspect of illness that is most destructive to the sick, I would choose the loss of control."[1]

One study appropriately entitled "Hardiness and Health" concluded,

> The control disposition is expressed as a tendency to feel and act as if one is influential (rather than helpless) in the face of the varied contingencies of life.... This does not imply the naive expectation of complete determination of events and outcomes but rather implies the perception of oneself as having a definite influence through the exercise of imagination, knowledge, skill, and choice...a sense of control.[2]

Another study by the same author discovered that those individuals who fared better when confronted with the stresses of life had the following traits: a strong commitment, a strong sense of having found meaning in their lives, and a sense that they were not just victims—that they could affect the outcome of their lives. They had the ability to recognize their distinctive values, goals, and priorities and they were aware of their capacity to make decisions and to find purpose in life.[3]

Other studies have shown that individuals who forfeit control over their future, sometimes even saying of their illness, "It's God's will," have a poorer prognosis. They tend to be fatalistic in their outlook. It's not surprising that they also feel helpless and hopeless.[4]

Not only do medical studies warn against placing yourself in the victim's role, the Bible itself does not commend a helpless "It's God's will" attitude toward illness. Christ praised the widow who fervently made her wishes known to Him; God extended the life of Hezekiah by 15 years after he prayed for healing. On the other hand, the Bible illustrates how Aaron's acquiescence resulted in tragedy for the Israelites. Eli's indulgence of his sons also exemplifies inappropriate passivity which yielded disastrous results. God did not leave men at the mercy of their natural environment, but "put him in charge of everything [He] made; everything is put under his authority."[5]

In order to increase the sense of control arthritis patients have over their own lives, the Stanford Arthritis Center devised a unique self-help program. They held sessions in which patients exchanged ideas and learned more about their illness. Then they were taught to manage their situation by designing their own treatment plan—choosing their own exercises and routines. The overall goal was to teach them to make decisions for themselves about their illness. The participants experienced a 35-percent reduction of pain, a 20-percent reduction of joint swelling, and an 18-percent reduction of depression. The article concluded that the reason for the improvement was the increase in knowledge of their disease, the change in attitude, and the greater degree of self-management.[6] More is being written all the time on the subject of the patient's role in his illness.

Take Responsibility for Your Treatment

One such book introduces the topic of the patient's role with these words: "This is a book about . . . healing and about how exceptional patients can take control in order to [assist in their own healing]."[7] Another book summarizes this topic by saying: "The basic theme of this book is that every person must accept a certain measure of responsibility for his or her own recovery from disease or disability."[8]

Assuming personal responsibility for the management of your illness means, first of all, taking an active role in the decision-making process. Patients need to learn that it is appropriate for them to ask questions about their diagnosis and the treatment options available. If there are lingering questions about the management of their illness, it is always proper to request a consultation with another physician. In more difficult medical situations, it is my policy to suggest to my patients that we get a second opinion. Getting another opinion cannot possibly hurt; if my diagnosis is confirmed, both the patient and I are reassured. If a different approach to treatment is recommended, I want to know that as much as my patient does. I don't know of any physician who has not been able to profit from another physician's opinion.

In our own situation, I have already elaborated about our efforts on behalf of Susan's getting the transplant. Another time we had to push her physician to get a second opinion. Many months after the transplant, Susan suffered with severe skin rashes and a general decrease in her sense of well-being. I thought it might be graft-versus-host disease, a reaction between the transplanted bone marrow and the recipient's body. Only after we put considerable pressure on her physician did he get another opinion, and the consultant quickly confirmed what I had suspected.

Unnoticed Opportunities for Control

Medical decisions constitute but one realm in which the patient can take control of his health. Untold opportunities for self-determination already exist in a person's life. A study of elderly nursing-home patients gave overwhelming evidence of the value of taking hold of these opportunities. The options that the patients already had at their disposal were pointed out to them, such as caring for plants and taking an active part in their daily activities. At the end of the 18-month study, this group of individuals was more alert, active, happy, social, as well as self-initiating and vigorous. They were twice as likely to be alive at the end of the study, as compared to a control group of comparable nursing-home residents who had the same options available to them but who were not encouraged to become actively involved.[9]

In conclusion, all our plans and dreams may be capsized, our bodies may be crippled, our emotions may rebel, and other people may betray us, yet still our will is free. It is free to take at least a limited amount of control in our lives, to hope for the good, to be kind to others, and to trust God amidst all the uncertainty and pain.

–13–

We Really Need Each Other

"I [Susan] found that the loss of control brought on by my illness and surroundings caused isolation and loneliness as well. When the people who visited me could take off their masks and leave after a few hours, they could never really understand how I felt being confined to a bed or room week after week.

"I was one of those fortunate ones whose hospital room overflowed with cards, posters, and balloons, while other rooms remained bare. Yet, in either environment, the patients feel isolated from healthy individuals who are free to control their lives. Though people surrounded me with well-meaning condolences and affection, often it didn't pierce my sense of aloneness.

"I found that a variety of circumstances can incubate loneliness and isolation. Both the physical surroundings and the malady itself can separate the individual from others. I observed many visitors' discomfort in the hospital room where I was surrounded by trays, tubes, IV pumps, and drab hospital bedding. Underneath their ill-fitting isolation gowns and masks the visitors often wondered, 'What is all this paraphernalia, and what should I say?' Some visitors related well to me, but others talked incessantly when I wished for quietness, joked when I was in a serious mood, or even barged in to pray for me in ways that I found offensive. Insensitivities like these tended to further isolate me emotionally. I know of one person whose way of handling this problem was to tell no one she had leukemia except her husband. Even after she broke down and told a few friends, she insisted no one put her name in the church bulletin or on the 'prayer chain' because she didn't want everyone calling to ask how she was. This patient cut off one of her most strategic channels to health—people.

"Though I was often tempted to withdraw, I worked hard at relating with people. When able, I would walk up and down the hallway pushing my IV pump and bottle, a hat covering my bald head. Even though I felt weak and uncommunicative, I tried to smile and initiate conversation with other patients. I found that talking to patients did the most to alleviate my sense of loneliness and isolation because they were the only ones who could truly understand how I felt. Moreover, I found that talking to other people took my mind off myself. Upon each successive hospitalization I renewed my commitment to treat those around me as *people*, not as tools for meeting my needs or merely as fixtures in the hospital environment.

"My family comes from stoic Scandinavian stock that tends to keep things in, and during my illness we were all tempted to pull back into ourselves. Fortunately, we learned to communicate at a deeper level than we ever had before. Also, John's warmth and acceptance helped me open up even more. Being able to share everything with him was life-sustaining for me.

"In addition, two women from my Sunday school class came to see me every week, the start of a friendship that has continued to this day. My church was phenomenal at keeping my family supplied with complete meals and sending hundreds of cards and notes, to name only a few of the ways they extended themselves socially and spiritually. My mom found help not only through some in-depth relationships, but also through an informative hospital support group."

Avoid Isolation at All Costs

As a physician I am aware that the medical literature is replete with the importance of avoiding isolation at all costs. This is something that every prisoner of war learned. Howard Ruttledge states in his book *In the Presence of Mine Enemies:* "The enemy knew that if he could isolate a man—make him feel abandoned—cut off—forgotten—he could more easily destroy his resistance and break down his morale."[1] In his book on human resilience, Dr. Julius Segal writes, "Many people who have successfully weathered staggering crises echo the same theme. Communication—even with only one person—offered them a lifeline for survival."

Segal goes on to say, "In every episode of captivity in recent American history POW's and hostages have been sustained by ingeniously improvised lifelines of communication." He quotes one POW he interviewed as saying, "The most important thing for survival as a POW was communication with someone, even if it was only a wave or a wink, a tap on a wall, or to have a guy put his thumb up. It made all the difference." This communication helped combat loneliness and despair and gave "strength to survive." In the course of his research, Dr. Segal found four reasons why communication is so helpful:

1) It is emotionally healing simply to put our feelings into words. 2) Communication helps us to recognize that others who faced similar problems managed to survive. 3) We learn through communication that our reactions to stress are not unnatural. 4) By choosing to interact with other people rather than withdrawing into ourselves, we are demonstrating a willingness to do something about our suffering—to control it.[2]

Expressing your feelings to other people not only has psychological benefits, but medical research has also shown it to facilitate physical healing. In one study of

women with breast cancer, those who "were communicative about their distress" survived longer. The study
concluded, "This body of research appears to establish a
consistent relationship: Cancer patients whose coping
styles facilitate external, conscious expression of negative emotions and psychological distress appear to survive longer."[3] Furthermore, studies of psychiatric patients and of medical students during exam time showed
a decrease in their immune function which was directly
related to their degree of loneliness.[4]

Social involvement in community and religious groups
has definitely been found to foster health and longevity.
One impressive study of 7000 people living in Alameda
County, California found that those who did not have
social ties were two-and-a-half times more likely to die
during the nine-year study than those with extensive
social ties. The study looked at the areas of marriage,
social ties, church membership, and informal group
associations. As the number of areas of involvement
increased, so did the life span of the individual.[5]

Even the involvement of caring for pets has been
shown to benefit a person's health. One study followed
a group of heart patients after their release from a coronary-care unit. One year later, 28 percent of those who
did not have pets had died, whereas only 3 percent of
those with pets had died. Other research indicates that
pets may help alleviate depression, solace loneliness,
facilitate personal growth, lower blood pressure, and
ease the pain of aging, as well as increase survivorship
from heart attacks.[6]

An article which appeared in *The American Journal of
Medicine* came to the following conclusion: "A Friend,
Not an Apple, a Day Will Help Keep the Doctor Away."[7]
It is no wonder that the Scriptures affirm that *we really
need each other*, telling us not to forsake the assembling of
ourselves together, but to encourage one another.[8]

-14-

To Accept the Things I Cannot Change

When Susan felt strong enough, she would wander U.C.L.A.'s floors pushing her IV pump everywhere she went and visit other patients. The following journal entry recounts a portion of one evening's meeting:

> Walking up and down the hall I saw a teen-aged guy, turned out his cousin has bone cancer. Talked with the patient's mom a long time. They're all Christians but I was disturbed by her militant attitude. "I'm expecting a miracle. I won't accept anything less." I think, "What happens to your life if you don't accept it if he dies or is crippled?" She talked a lot about faith but she also said she's been angry at God. ... What a bundle of contradictions she presented!

If the woman's son dies, Susan found herself wondering, will she have a nervous breakdown? Will she reject God? Will her bitterness poison the lives of her family?

One chapter of *Where Is God When It Hurts?* tells of a family that has not fully accepted their situation, yet seems to have avoided being bitter and rejecting God. Brian S. was training to compete as a gymnast in the 1964 Olympics. But he landed on his head during a trampoline jump, breaking his neck and dashing all his dreams as an athlete. Not only is he paralyzed, but he also has excruciating pain which torments him daily. Even though he has been this way for a decade, he and his family are still seeking a miracle. His mother gave the following explanation:

> I never read about Jesus saying to a blind man, "Sorry, buddy, I wish I could help, but God is trying to teach you something, so get used to it." When Jesus saw a blind man, He healed. . . .
>
> I have no idea when God will heal Brian. . . .
>
> Brian is the first to admit the progress he has made. But now more than ever, he does not accept his condition. He has one hope and one prayer—for total healing.[1]

When to Accept

In an earlier chapter I told of my brother's martyrdom. The dramatic story of the trumped-up charges against him and the threats to execute him were repeatedly on radio, TV, and newspapers, and it was a cover article of both *Time* and *Life* magazines. We received numerous phone calls, including ones from the office of the president of the United States and Billy Graham. Literally millions of people around the world were praying for Paul's deliverance from the Congolese rebels. Some people told us of having had visions from God that he would be unharmed, but he was killed.

During the three months of his imprisonment, we prayed earnestly for Paul's deliverance but never had an inward assurance of his release. God seemed to be preparing us for the possibility of his death. Many people struggled after Paul's "senseless" death, but with God's preparation, acceptance was much easier for Betty and me.

The Scriptures repeatedly encourage us to pray. However, just because we ask for healing does not guarantee that healing will inevitably occur. God is not limited in

His power to heal, but two factors do affect His actions on our behalf: 1) His overall plan and purpose for the universe and 2) the choices of men. Not every person in the Bible who asked for healing was healed. The apostle Paul prayed three times for deliverance from an infirmity, but he wasn't delivered of it. Even Christ's prayer the night before the crucifixion that the "cup" of His suffering and death be taken away was not granted. He still suffered an excruciating execution.[2]

Although prayer is exceedingly powerful, it in fact has God-ordained limits. Likewise, we humanly can do a great deal to alter the course of a disease, but the realm of our control also has its limits. This theme is echoed in the book *The Healing Brain*: "We should view health as a constant battle between the strength of the attack and the stability of the defense. The patient is neither always responsible for the disease nor always helpless."[3]

The author of *The Healer Within* quotes Dr. Barrie Cassileth who expressed concern that overemphasizing our own power can create problems:

> There is a danger to the notion, the yet unproven notion, that one's mind can affect something as biologically overwhelming as an advanced malignant disease. The danger is that if patients buy into the idea that if they only think the right way they will cure their cancers and, in some instances, they fail to be cured, they then assume a burden of guilt and blame for having failed to cure themselves.[4]

Thus, it is my belief that in certain situations we must accept what is happening to us. Most of this book discusses resisting illness, but this chapter deals with the time and place to appropriately accept our situation. A prayer attributed to Saint Francis of Assisi beautifully expresses such acceptance:

God grant me the serenity
to accept the things I cannot change,
the courage to change the things I can,
and the wisdom to know the difference.

Putting Acceptance into Practice

How do we put this prayer into practice? Every situation is so different. Can we find any guidelines that apply to all of them? Our suffering may be in the area of our health, our finances, or our relationships, and it always affects our emotions. Health problems may force us to deal with the thought of impending death; they may debilitate us with progressive diseases such as Cystic Fibrosis or Alzheimer's disease; or they may inflict us with chronic suffering such as Rheumatoid Arthritis or severe back problems. Sometimes suffering comes in the form of coping with loss whether it be the loss of a house, a limb, or our reputation. Other times the suffering involves an ongoing relationship, such as the day-in, day-out struggle it takes to make a troubled marriage work.

While there are indeed many types of suffering, one thing every illness, loss, or misfortune has in common is that each one requires the person to adapt in some way if he is to cope successfully. A change has come into your life, and you too must change. The first step in adaptation is to assess the situation by answering this question: What aspects of my situation do I have control over and what aspects do I have to accept? Once you have determined what is under your control and what is not, the "givens" of your situation must be accepted, which means that you learn to live with them.

The following are some examples of givens. In relationship problems, it is crucial to realize that you cannot change the other person. You may decide to confront him and to talk to him about the problem, but only the other person can actually change himself.

Some suffering has very obvious "givens." An amputee cannot grow a new arm. A widow cannot bring her husband back to life. While accepting life without a limb or life without a mate cannot be expected to happen in a day, a great deal of healing begins the moment the reality of the loss is accepted. The arm is gone; the husband is gone. There can be nothing more "given" than that. The givens of your situation must be accepted so that you can start going on with your life.

Undoubtedly the most difficult aspect of an illness that might have to be accepted is the fact that a person will never be healed. One of my dilemmas before the possibility of the transplant came into being was over how much painful treatment I should encourage in an effort to prolong Susan's life. At what point would we have to accept the fact that the leukemia would kill her? Fortunately, we did not have to answer that question. But many do. Similarly, I believe that there is a point when the paralyzed person must set aside his hopes of walking and concentrate on developing his remaining muscles.

Yet another area in which we need acceptance is that of our physical limitations. The person recovering from a serious illness, the invalid, and the handicapped must learn to pace themselves in their activities, working at adapting to their limitations.

Accepting your limitations does not necessarily mean you have a lack of faith. It does not mean you have given up your confidence in God's omnipotence, goodness, or desire to make you healthy and whole. Instead, you are deciding to trust God in the midst of an undesirable situation.

Neither is acceptance to be construed as resignation. Resignation views the circumstances as inevitable, holding on to anger or hopelessness. Resignation gives up; it has lost sight of any hope, and denies even the possibility that there might be meaning in the situation.

Acceptance always brings with it hope and gives the person a sense of meaning in the midst of uncertainty.

So the underlying given is that life is difficult. Scott Peck states in *The Road Less Traveled* that most of us do not want to face this fact. Instead, we complain incessantly about the enormity of our problems as if life should be easy. He emphasizes that once we accept this fact, then life is no longer as difficult.[5]

Another given to accept is following the necessary medical treatment. As a physician I see some patients who constantly resist needed treatment, thus making their problem many times worse than it need be. One patient begrudgingly came in to see me for several years, continually resistant to taking the antidepressant medication she desperately needed. I occasionally would say to her, only half joking, "Once you accept the fact that you need to see a psychiatrist and have to take medication, you probably won't need to come in very often and need very much medication." She struggled several more years with fairly severe depression before accepting her situation, at which time my prediction proved to be true—and she made dramatic improvement thereafter.

Acceptance Necessitates Forgiveness

In order to fully accept we must forgive. Living in the age of God's permissive will, as discussed in previous chapters, results in the possibility of our suffering from the careless or hurtful actions of other people. We may even be blamed by individuals for things we have not done. Such injustices frequently cause us to react in destructive ways. We hold grudges, sulk, wallow in self-pity, become bitter and resentful, and may even seek revenge. Whatever the manifestation may be, when we resist forgiving other people for the hurts they have inflicted on us, we pay an enormous emotional price.

On the other hand, forgiving them brings tremendous healing.

The noted Christian writer Catherine Marshall tells of a friend who almost died when his mentally unstable roommate attacked him with a knife, stabbing him over and over again. Mercifully, the man finally stopped and ran out of the apartment. Lying there motionless to keep his lungs from filling with blood, somehow the victim was able to forgive his attacker and experienced peace. He was rushed to the hospital in critical condition. After his long and arduous recovery he thanked the doctor for saving his life. The physician corrected him by saying:

> No-o. There's another reason [you're alive]. Your condition has been so precarious that anything could have tipped the scales. . . .
>
> You've been at peace with yourself, especially the last ten days. If you had held on to any hate at all, that negative emotion would have sapped so much of your energy that you probably would not have pulled through.[6]

Forgiving doesn't mean the other person didn't wrong you. Nor does it say you don't hurt. Forgiveness means ceasing to hold the wrong against the other person. The Amplified Version of Matthew 6:14,15 expresses it well:

> For if you forgive people their trespasses— that is, their reckless and willful sins, leaving them, letting them go and giving up resentment—your heavenly Father will also forgive you.
>
> But if you do not forgive others their trespasses—their reckless and willful sins, leaving them, letting them go and giving up resentment—neither will your Father forgive you your trespasses.

Howard Ruttledge wrote after returning from seven years in a North Vietnamese prison, "Revenge is God's business. Anger and hatred can destroy us all. When it's over, we must try to forget and to forgive."[7]

Forgiveness not only means forgiving other people, but "forgiving" God. This is not to say that God has done anything wrong, but most of us in the midst of deep suffering charge God with not running the universe right, at least our particular part of the universe. We need to drop our charges against Him and accept what He is allowing to happen in our lives. Suffering has rightfully been called God's megaphone to get our attention; God repeatedly uses it to make us stop and think about how we are living our lives and what our relationship is with our Maker.

-15-

The Healing Power of Hope

"When I [Susan] first heard that I had Acute Myelogenous Leukemia one thought monopolized my mind—'I don't want to be dead in five years.' Months later, during my first remission, this thought had subsided somewhat, only to be replaced by a haunting, ever-present sense of uncertainty. Knowing that I could relapse any time, I wrote in my journal:

> [I am] struggling with [the question of] how do I live a normal life and plan for the future while the possibility of sickness and death at any time looms over me. . . . I decided that sort of constant uncertainty is the worst of it all.

"And so not only did the diagnosis breed despair, but also the treatment and the uncertainty of the results.

"The following year one bone marrow test shattered all my hopes for a cure. The leukemia had come back. Medically speaking, there was no longer any possibility of a cure—the best that could be done was to prolong my life through chemotherapy. My physician told John that even if the treatment was effective, the best we could hope for was a two- to three-month remission. And he told my mother that without a remission, I would live about two to 12 weeks. Sometimes I would see my father cry like a baby when that fact penetrated his defenses.

"Lying in my hospital bed a few days later, it all started to hit me. Would I ever get out of the hospital again, feel the ocean breeze, or hear the waves roar? Even if I did get a second remission and get out of the hospital, would I ever be strong enough to enjoy the freedom of a bike ride or the challenge of a full-time job? Would John and I ever be able to get married? My heart started to pound as these thoughts raced through my head, and with each rapid heartbeat, each monotonous rotation of the IV pump, fear pulsed through me.

"I was beginning to realize that throughout the previous year of my illness much of my hope had been placed in my youth and physical fitness, my strong will and positive outlook, the top-notch doctors, and the fact that the disease had been caught early. It had been relatively easy for me to get my first remission, and humanly speaking, if anyone's first remission should have resulted in a cure, it should have been mine. At that point I realized that though all of these qualities were useful, more than ever now the focus of my hope would have to be in God.

"After ten days of intensive chemotherapy depleted my white count to practically zero, I shivered and sweated through weeks of 104- to 105-degree fevers. Sometimes I hallucinated and talked aloud to people who weren't in the room. Nothing could bring down my fever, not even the loathsome ice blanket. My body shook with chills and my teeth chattered constantly, completely exhausting me, and through it all, the nausea and vomiting from the chemotherapy continued. These circumstances drained me of all my hope.

"Another source of discouragement was the lack of hope expressed by my doctors during the first year of treatment. They would talk about trying to get a remission but would never even mention the word 'cure.' My parents wondered if my doctor emphasized the worst prognosis because he felt a need to protect us from getting our hopes up and being let down. For a person who was struggling, these were not the most hopeful of circumstances.

"Fortunately, I had a second remission. But since we had no idea how long it would be, John and I immediately began to plan our wedding.

"I can still remember the evening two days before my wedding, sitting in my favorite easy chair in the living room as I was writing out my vows. I had thought out all the ideas before, so it was an easy and enjoyable task. Yet a lump formed in my throat as I thought of the traditional vows, '. . . in sickness and health. . . .' We've already had the sickness part, I *hope* we get some of the health. I continued thinking about the vows. '. . .'Til death do us part. . . .' In other words, until I die, I thought with sadness. But I wanted to trust God, and we were asking for a long life. So I would hope for that. I decided to end my vows with, 'as long as God allows me to live.' I remember saying those words with tears in my eyes as I held John's hands. I felt that same sadness mixed with hopeful trust, while enveloped by the love and elation that characterized our wedding day."

Hope Springs from Despair

The medical situation in which Susan found herself seemed completely hopeless. Individuals with a variety of problems—the person who just lost his job, the woman whose husband has left, or the young couple whose baby has a birth defect—share similar feelings. The first reaction is virtually always despair. They feel like they have just stepped off a cliff and don't know how to fight the hopelessness that pulls them down like gravity. However, from the Scriptures it is clear that true hope springs out of the depths of despair. "But hope that is seen is not hope. . . . But if we hope for what we do not see, with perseverance we wait eagerly for it."[1]

Medical research also supports the fact that hope springs from hopelessness. One journal says that "hope begins when personal resources are exhausted" and another states: "Hope has its true beginnings only in a situation that tempts one to despair."[2] Another journal states, "Hope, then, is a derivative, a force that comes to birth out of the pains of despair, *and it would not arise otherwise.* . . . If reality does not first give us reasons for despairing, it cannot give us grounds for hoping."[3] One psychiatrist found that the most important ingredient needed to survive the Nazi death camps was "blind, naked hope," which he defined as being the kind of hope a person has to have when, humanly speaking, he can see no reason to hope.[4]

In a recent medical journal, a physician who had attended a conference of the American Society of Medical Oncology wrote that he had overheard two cancer specialists discussing papers they had presented the day before:

> One was complaining bitterly. "You know, Bob, I just don't understand it. We used the same drugs, the same dosage, the same schedule and the same entry criteria. Yet I got a 22 percent response rate and you got a 74 percent. That's unheard of for [widespread] lung cancer. How do you do it?"
>
> "We're both using Etoposide, Platinol, Oncovin, and Hydroxyurea. You call yours EPOH. I tell my patients I'm giving them HOPE. Sure, I tell them it's experimental . . . but I emphasize that we have a chance."
>
> "Aren't you giving them false hope with that approach?"
>
> He said gently, "Don't you give them false despair when you stress only the side effects of the treatment and the grimness of the prognosis?"[5]

This doctor who tries to give his patients hope would probably agree with Norman Cousin's advice, "You never deny the diagnosis, but do deny the verdict that goes with it."[6]

The fortifying power of hope has also been proven with animals. In one experiment wharf rats were put into water and sprayed. For awhile they fought to stay alive, then, after an average of 17 minutes, they gave up and drowned. Another group of wharf rats was then given the same treatment. But just before they drowned, after about 17 minutes, they were pulled from the water, dried off, and restored to normal health. Sometime later they were put back into a similar tub of water and this time they fought for 35 hours before drowning.[7]

So hope increases a person's will to fight for life. In addition, there is more and more medical evidence that demonstrates the positive effect hope has on a person's body chemistry and immune system.[8] Despair or hopelessness has been shown to increase the death toll after cardiac surgery and speed the growth of a cancer. Hope, on the other hand, has been positively correlated with regressions or cures of cancers; it is known to decrease postoperative complications, to name only a few of the well-established medical benefits.

One of the authors of *The Healing Brain* made this observation about his own suffering: "Despair was easy but hope required continued effort. I think this is because hope implies uncertainty about the future and the brain finds it difficult to maintain a state of uncertainty. Despair at least offers the troubled mind certainty and stability."[9] And so the pattern we see over and over again is that despair is easy but hope is hard. Unless we fight it, the mind tends to gravitate toward despair.

Hopelessness has been described as inaction in the face of a threat. It has been contrasted with hope, which causes a person to "act, achieve, move and plan futuristically and assertively."[10] By definition, hope means not only longing for something, but also expecting or believing in its fulfillment. Hope has been referred to as "a window on the future."[11] E. Stanley Jones was a well-known evangelist whose very life was a demonstration of hope—of what he called the "Divine Yes"—saying "yes" to God and "yes" to life. In his last book, written at 88 years of age despite a crippling stroke, he gave one of the secrets of his life of hope: "I have learned that if you are blocked on one road in life, you can always find another that will open up for you."[12] God gave a similar reason for hope to the nation of Israel when He promised He would transform her "Valley of Troubles into a Door of Hope."[13]

Hope and despair are a matter of someone's focus. The despairing person looks at his life and only focuses on the negative things, even if the positives far outweigh the negatives. He looks ahead and can see only negative outcomes when, in reality, positive outcomes are equally probable. When I encouraged a patient of mine to look at his life more positively—like a glass that is half-full instead of half-empty—he retorted, "But the water in my glass is filled with arsenic."

In contrast, the person with hope looks at his life and focuses on the positive aspects of it; he looks at the future and sees the potential for good outcomes. This principle is exemplified in the Scriptures: "I would have despaired unless I had believed that I would see the goodness of the Lord in the land of the living."[14]

Nurturing Hope "In the Land of the Living"

What then are some practical steps someone can apply to nurture hope? Probably the best starting point for anybody who is trying to hope is to search for a positive image of the future, something that is very tangible and very real to him. In his book *A Gift of Hope*, Robert Veninga wrote the following: "How do you summon the courage to love life when surrounded by gloom? You search and search and search. Until you find *one person, one idea,* one avocation that is so powerful that it penetrates the gloom." It has been found that children who gallantly survived horrible circumstances would latch on to "any excuse for hope and faith in recovery."[15]

Stress expert Shlomo Bresnitz wrote that hope takes energy: "It means finding something to build on—an unthinkable task if your energies are consumed by remorse. . . . 'One has to . . . tell oneself some stories with happy endings.' "[16] Veninga also affirms that one way to control panic is "by ceasing to dwell on your fears or dreary prognoses or feelings that you can never again be happy or well. And in their place you find reasons for hope."[17] Doctors Ornstein and Sobel say in *The Healing Brain*:

> The normal strategies of the mind's operating system—simplification, exclusion of information—make us continually overreact from the little information we finally do select and allow to enter our consciousness. . . .
>
> The contents of the mind at any moment are automatically overemphasized no matter how they get there.[18]

Thus when we select to look at the glass as "half-empty" we tend to amplify that view so that it is all we see—there is no water in the glass. We then believe it and act on it—as if it were true. We, however, can just as appropriately choose to view the glass as "half-full," thereby emphasizing the positive and having the benefits thereof.

Generally, we all tend to become hopeless when some dream of ours is dashed. In the process we often compare ourselves with other people who have what we want. We see their perfect health, happy marriage, wealth, or ideal children. We often are not aware of their struggles. As we compare ourselves with those people who seem to have more, we despair. Instead, we may do well to look at the many who have so much less: the mentally deficient, the sick with pain every waking second, the patient who struggles and still cannot get a full breath of air, the starving in Africa, the homeless bag lady, or the individual who has no faith in God. Out of this perspective we can start to see the many things God has blessed us with, the "half-full glass."

In struggling to apply the principles that I have been describing, Susan relates:

"At some point, I finally had to accept the fact that I would never know complete peace and certainty until I entered eternity with God; that life on this earth always has its share of uncertainty. Nevertheless, if I were to get through the agonizing hospitalizations, I needed something *tangible* to hang on to—some positive image of the future to focus on. Being healed so I could live my life with John became one of my strongest sources of hope. As I wrote in my journal, 'Knowing that John does need me, and loving him and wanting the most benefit and pleasure for him, I want to live and thus be there for John. . . . Lord, I ask for life in which we point many people to You and demonstrate Your love in our love for each other.'

"I found that in order to focus on the positive, I also had to stop focusing on the negative. This was a lesson that I had to keep coming back to. During treatment for the second remission, I was looking forward to going home. I set my mind against thinking at all about returning to the hospital. I remember one morning a day or two before leaving the hospital, in came a well-meaning physician who started to talk about when I would return for future chemotherapy. I quickly interjected, 'Don't say a word to me about coming back in here!' I knew deep inside that I would do what was medically advisable. But I chose not to think about the negative aspects of my horrible plight at that time. I also tried not to think ahead about goals that I feared I would never see accomplished. I felt that wondering whether I would be disappointed in the future would spoil my enjoyment of whatever health a remission might give me. Instead, John and I decided to get married as soon as possible. On the evening of my discharge from the hospital, we set a wedding date for only ten days away. Our Hawaiian honeymoon was like a fantasy amidst a nightmare. I was able to fully enjoy a one-month reprieve before returning for the transplant.

"I discovered a vivid example of the 'glass being half-full instead of half-empty' with my low white blood counts. Before my father's bone marrow was injected into me, my own bone marrow was completely annihilated by chemotherapy and radiation. In order for me to live, my father's marrow had to engraft into my bones and produce healthy cells. I was required to stay in protective isolation until the new cells were formed and my blood count reached the magic number of 500 granulocytes. The body normally has about 4000 granulocytes, or 'fighter' white cells. After the transplant, it took eight weeks for this count to reach 500. Each day after I heard the results of my blood tests, I found that when I focused on what I did not have—the 500 granulocytes—I found myself despairing. When I gratefully and joyfully accepted the God-given gifts I did have, I was able to trust, praise, and hope.

"It Won't Last Forever"

"Along this line, another phrase that helped give me hope was, 'It won't last forever.' I need to be cautious of using this phrase, though, for it may not be comforting to many. During my relapse, if anybody had said to me, 'It won't last forever,' it probably would have been received with, 'But I don't *know* that! I'm afraid it *will* be forever—at least for the rest of my life.' But later on, 'It won't last forever' became a source of hope for me. I was comforted by remembering that though the pain of the moment seemed interminable, it wasn't. It seemed unbearable—but it never was. Only four weeks into my ten-week hospital stay, I remember feeling like I had been in there forever. But now looking back on it, I only see a blur with about a week's worth of memories.

"During the nine months it took to recover from the transplant, 'It won't last forever' turned out to be one of my best sources of hope and my best coping strategy. I had to deal with regular, uncontrollable vomiting, which nothing would stop except falling asleep. I finally learned to bring my basin, glass of water, mouthwash, and pillow out to the living room and curl up in front of the TV. It wasn't so bad if I accepted the fact that I just had to go through one more bout of it; the sooner I could fall asleep, the sooner it would be over; it would end—it always had before. In other words, 'It won't last forever.'

Faith, the Source of Hope

"In the Bible I found three great chapters on faith and hope. In Hebrews 10, I was encouraged to remember the difficult times I had weathered in the past when I read 'recall the former days when . . . you endured a hard struggle with sufferings. . . . Therefore do not throw away your confidence, which has a great reward.' This proved to be a significant source of hope for me. In chapter 11, I was challenged by the way others had encountered and mastered their difficult circumstances through their faith in God. Then in chapter 12, I was comforted and inspired as I saw how Christ had endured such suffering for me. Thus God's Word gave me hope.

Eternal Hope

"What about the person who has not gotten a remission, who is steadily losing weight, and is facing the terror of death? Is there hope when there is no hope? No discussion of this topic would be complete if this question were not answered.

"I found that in order to make it through, I needed more than something on this earth on which to set my hopes. Though John and I were deeply in love and this gave me a strong incentive to live, I needed something more than that. I had to have an eternal hope. The Bible calls this the strongest hope of all: 'This hope we have as an anchor of the soul, a hope both sure and steadfast.'[19] In my journal I wrote the following:

> And as that [constant uncertainty] gnawed at me and I tried to find a place for it, it dawned on me that all uncertainty will be banished only in heaven. And I wanted that peace. At that moment, and still, when I really think of it, such perfect peace is something I want, something heavenly. (I've never wanted to go to heaven before—life here is plenty fine!) ... Now, *personally* it makes no difference whether I live or die. That's from God. That's strange and unnatural, yet calm.

"Having an eternal hope brings great peace to our daily lives, for it helps put our problems in perspective. Noted theologian A.W. Tozer wrote in his book *The Knowledge of the Holy*, 'The man who comes to a right belief about God is relieved of ten thousand temporal problems, for he sees at once that these have to do with matters which at the most cannot concern him for very long.'[20] One of the most difficult yet crucial concepts for us to grasp is that this life and the suffering we go through in it is only a fleeting moment in time when compared to eternity. In addition, God assures us we will be more than rewarded for the pain we have gone through in this life. The apostle Paul writes: 'The sufferings of this present time are not worthy to be compared with the glory which shall be revealed in us.' In another letter, he calls our suffering a light affliction in comparison to heaven's joys: 'Our light affliction, which is but for a moment, worketh for us a far more exceeding and eternal weight of glory.'[21]

"Having an eternal perspective does not mean that we lose our desire for life on earth. When I experienced a desire for heaven during my illness, I was scared because it seemed to imply that I was losing my desire to live. Even when I found myself writing in my journal about this desire for heaven, I immediately countered it by adding the words, 'No, I want to live!' But now it was a different desire. It was no longer an anxious, out-of-control clutching at life; there was a calm and a peace in the desire. I found that having an eternal perspective didn't take away my desire to live; rather, it gave me a deep security in God that freed me to thoroughly and gratefully enjoy the life I had, even during hospitalizations and difficult recuperations."

–16–

Laughter, Praise, and Joy

There was one prominent finding in a study of 24 outstanding ministers: The one characteristic they all had in common was a sense of humor. "The reason is clear; these pulpit giants know who is in charge of the world, that God will win out in the end."[1] One is often more able to laugh when he can see his circumstances—even suffering—from God's perspective.

Laughter, praise, and joy may seem incongruent to many, but all three spring from a sense of hopefulness. The person who draws comfort from God's assurances can praise Him and be joyful. That person also has the objectivity to laugh at himself and his foibles. Studies that have followed individuals who have grown up in adverse situations and done exceedingly well show, among other characteristics, a wide range of emotions "including capacity for fun, joy... play, and creativity."[2] As one medical article points out, "Hopeful people laugh more than hopeless ones."[3]

Laughter

Laughter, as well as praise and joy, not only indicates emotional health, but actually contributes to the emotional and physical healing process. In recent years, Norman Cousins popularized the current interest in laughter for treating disease. His book tells about his use of humor to overcome a serious arthritic condition. He says, "I made a joyous discovery that ten minutes of genuine belly laughter had an anesthetic effect and would give me at least two hours of pain-free sleep." This notion is not new, however. Viktor Frankl spoke of humor as "another of the soul's weapons in the fight for self preservation" in the Nazi concentration camps. In 1790 the philosopher Kant said that jokes nurture the vital bodily processes and generate a "favorable influence on health." Three thousand years ago Solomon said, "A cheerful heart is good medicine." Recent studies have confirmed that humor does actually enhance a person's immune system. Lasting benefit, however, requires that the individual incorporate humor into his lifestyle.[4]

On this subject Susan relates the following:

"I tend to be a reserved, somewhat introverted person who takes things seriously. Through the months of illness I became more aware of the benefit of breaking tension or lightening an awkward situation with a joke. On the day-to-day level, I found it much more beneficial to look for reasons to laugh than to allow the giant life-and-death issues to consume me.

"I looked for ways to infuse humor into my sterile environment. In some rooms I had a portable covered commode—it looked more like a wheelchair—which served as a seat for visitors when chairs were in short supply. The looks on people's faces when they found out what they were sitting on and, occasionally, that it needed to be emptied, provided humor on more than one occasion! Once I wound up a little toy and placed it in a box of Q-tips so it started running when my nurse pulled some out. It startled him at first but then gave him quite a laugh. I read Garfield comic books, and my dad would always bring up the Sunday funnies, which I would save to read in the evening with John. They seemed twice as funny with him. In fact, to this day we save the Sunday funnies and read them together in bed at night.

"Some evenings I felt better and visitors could help with humor. Two faithful friends, Linda Hibst and Kathy Brawley, often lifted my spirits this way. One night they brought Pepsi, potato chips, vanilla wafers, and video tapes of *Blazing Saddles* and a Johnny Carson anniversary show. We made complete pigs of ourselves, laughing away with our feet up on the extra chairs. We learned how to put straws behind a mask or cut a slit in it for the straw. Cookies and chips could be quickly popped behind the mask—often a hilarious sight!

"Late at night, we would often 'go on a safari' together: I wore a pith helmet and, pushing the old IV pump, we stalked the hallways in search of adventure, wary of any 'unknown dangers' lurking behind the 'No Admission' signs in the 'uncharted back territory' of the hospital. 'Adventure' usually meant teasing and joking with my nurses.

"In ways like these I made a conscious effort to develop a sense of humor; for me it doesn't come naturally. Sometimes I could only laugh if I viewed a situation the way I would if I were telling about it at a party a year later. How anyone could avoid being crushed by such months in the hospital without learning to laugh is beyond me.

Praise and Joy

"Just as I worked at developing a sense of humor, there were times that praise required a conscious effort. During the six-week hospitalization after my recurrence, I found that praise doesn't have to be spontaneous for it to be beneficial. That hospital stay was absolutely the lowest point of my life, both emotionally and physically. One morning, I wrote in my journal:

> I wake up so ill-at-ease! I feel like I'm starting on a headache already. I want to wake up praising God, entrusting the day to Him, optimistic and eager to see what He will bring to pass during that day. But my just-waking prayers

like that are mechanical and there's nothing I can do to change my spirit, Lord! YOU change it—please!

I am praising you singing 'Bless the Lord, O my soul...' but it's not joyous. I feel like David's remembering how he used to go to the temple in grief because he felt 'God has turned his back on him.' You don't [turn Your back on us]. I know that. I know You're here—no doubts there. And I know You are trustworthy and You will restore my joy. I'll just wait.

Lord, I praise You—feeling or no feeling. I will praise You—with tears in my eyes....

So, Lord, here I am. Take me in Your arms and alter my attitude. Mend my heart. You will.

"While suffering, I have learned that praising God is, to a great extent, an act of obedience, at least initially. However, rejoicing does not mean faking joy or hiding our pain. It does not mean that we parrot the words 'Praise the Lord!' I would feel I was being dishonest with myself if I used 'Praise the Lord!' to camouflage my feelings, and I found that I was very irritated by visitors who seemed to do so or implied that I should do the same. Instead, I had to say something like, 'I know God is good, though right now it doesn't seem like He is,' or 'I feel terrible but I want to praise God anyway.'

"Though the weeks of terribly high fevers and the fear of never again being healthy left me completely exhausted and miserable, I had tremendous moments of joy and worship. For a relief from the ice blanket, I would turn it off and have my mom rub my back with cold water or alcohol to cool my body. I would play tapes of Christian music and just worship, singing along in my mind. Because I was placing all of my trust in God, my worship and experience of the joy and peace of His presence transcended my circumstances. Times like these, during my relapse, surpassed any worship and joy I have known, before or since.

"If I had to choose the single-most transcendent worship experience I had, it would undoubtedly be the time at the New Year's Eve Family Communion in 1985, the night before my hospitalization for the relapse. However, I had many similar experiences during that hospitalization. These were not times when I felt that 'God was right beside me' as someone asked. That would put my focus on God's comforting *me*. Me and my situation were completely irrelevant during those times. I was fully aware of my wretched condition physically and psychologically, but my attention was entirely focused on God: His glory, His awesome power, love, goodness, and majesty. It wasn't that everything else didn't matter or that I felt insignificant; other things did matter and I knew God loved me deeply. But those thoughts didn't even enter my mind—worshiping God simply transcended all else. It's no wonder that the Scripture says 'The joy of the Lord is your strength.'[5]

"I found that when I admitted my real feelings and then focused on God's character, genuine feelings of praise and thanks would well up within me. I wrote:

> Two weeks—I'm sick of being in here—sick of medicine and slow interns and fevers and being too weak to read. Sick of tape on my body being pulled off and not being able to eat. I don't feel like I even remember how it is to really enjoy food! Complain, complain. . . .
>
> Yet I have so much to be thankful for—so much love being poured out on me—John, family, church—people I don't even know. I want to keep an attitude of praise.

"I would ask God to teach me how to rejoice, then read psalms and listen to hymns of praise. Sometimes writing down or making a mental note of answered prayer or positive events in my life, no matter how small, brought about genuine thanksgiving. I found that marveling at God's creation and grandeur became the most hopeful way I could occupy my mind at a time when so many worries were clamoring for my attention. By seeking ways to praise God in the midst of overwhelming difficulties, I found an eternal hope that carried me through my day-to-day pain."

-17-

Suffering with Purpose
and Meaning

Temporal Meaning

Great thinkers down through the centuries have come to the conclusion that we need to find purpose in the midst of our suffering. Brother Lawrence, a monk in the seventeenth century, said, "The sorest afflictions never appear intolerable, except when we see them in the wrong light."[1] Three centuries later, Victor Frankl concurred, "Suffering ceases to be suffering in some way at the moment it finds a meaning . . . man is even ready to suffer, on the condition, to be sure, that his suffering has a meaning."[2] More recently, studies have shown that "a fundamental sense of purpose" is the single most important means of resisting stress.[3] Similarly, the survivors of the Nazi death camps were those who held on to a sense of purpose.[4]

Discovering purpose and meaning in suffering takes many forms. For some, such as Nazi prisoners, it has meant having a reason to live, such as finding and being reunited with a family member. For others, such as the World War II soldiers who needed less pain medication than civilians with comparable wounds, it involved believing that their suffering was for a worthy cause.[5] These individuals were able to endure great pain because they believed either that their suffering had a meaningful cause or that they had a reason to endure it.

Unfortunately, the cause of someone's pain, the purpose or the reason to persevere through a terrible situation, often are not readily apparent to the sufferer.

Nevertheless, the person who believes that good will triumph and that life has meaning even during suffering can act on the basis of that belief. A person's choices and actions during suffering can transform the seemingly random, purposeless situations into meaningful ones. Frankl speaks of this type of meaning in suffering:

> The way in which a man accepts his [situation] and all the suffering it entails, the way in which he takes up his cross, gives him ample opportunity—even under the most difficult circumstances—to add a deeper meaning to his life. He may remain brave, dignified and unselfish. Or in the bitter fight for self-preservation he may forget his human dignity and become no more than an animal.[6]

Bearing suffering with dignity and humanity, seeing it as potentially meaningful, requires that a person progress through the earlier stages we discussed. The person mired down with anger and bitterness cannot begin to see meaning in the situation because it would necessitate his giving up the anger which consumes all his energy. Other people devote themselves to the process of denial or to desperate attempts at bargaining their way out of the difficulty. A person must find the courage to work through the unpleasant issues, take appropriate action, and have hope. Only then is he free to start looking for meaning in the situation.

Most of the time, an individual can take a first step toward finding purpose by choosing to reach out to other people in some way, however small. Susan saw that compassion can replace the negative feelings. Concern for other people can start to alleviate some of our own pain and actually contribute to healing. As God begins to comfort us, we will in turn be enabled to reach out and comfort others.[7] The process becomes a circle:

We work through our pain and begin to see purpose in it as God comforts us. Then we reach out to others and find meaning in helping them. This action and meaning brings further healing and the capacity to give still more.

Susan tells about how she found this principle to be true:

"I don't think I could have tolerated my illness if I didn't believe that some good could come out of it. So I tried to be useful, even while in the hospital. I would visit other patients and try to be an encouragement to them and to the nurses.

"Although caring for others gave me a sense of usefulness, I drew a deeper sense of purpose from the fact that I had to and could depend on God for my very life. I rejoiced in His presence and the fact that *He* loved and cared for me—a fact I was so much more aware of because of my own impotence. When I returned to school after my remission I had a different struggle: to depend on God even when healthy. I wrote in my journal:

> [I noticed] such a change in the quality of [my] life from the six months in and out of the hospital. I don't want 'normal life' to lessen my sense of complete dependence on God. Whether I'm mostly resting and doing homework, or visiting with people, or teaching I want '*For me to live is Christ*' to apply and to love Him such that I know '*to die is gain*.' This verse gives *meaning* to my life.

"The year following my transplant, I continued to cling to that verse as one that offered meaning, even during those days and weeks when all I was doing was surviving—when it was a morning's task to fix myself a bowl of Cream of Wheat.

"Though I was a newlywed, I could do very little work around our new apartment. I made it a goal, however, to be a supportive, active listener to John when he came home from work. I made my struggles a motivation for later doing an in-depth personal Bible study, which I subsequently was asked to teach.

"I saw God use that Bible study in other people's lives. But I was humbled: I couldn't take the credit for the principles I was learning. God had changed my heart during those months that I had to depend on Him. He began transforming me as I worked on focusing more on my relationship with God than on what I could accomplish. My ease in telling God my feelings and desires and my confidence that He cares and *does* act on my behalf has grown tremendously. Also, I now appreciate the awesome resources of peace and joy available through truly worshiping God.

"For the most part, the lessons were learned and the changes took place when—according to the world's standards—I was powerless, unable to be useful. I gradually came to realize that doing useful things is not necessarily the same as having a purpose or meaning. During healthy times I have sometimes felt purposeless while frantically active and productive. On the other hand, I believe my life and my suffering had meaning even when I could do nothing but shiver with fevers and feel afraid. I still loved and wanted to serve God and *He* had the power to bring good out of it all.

"During my slow recovery from the transplant I began to put into practice my belief that ultimately the meaning of a situation comes from God, not from the useful things I did myself. I had to learn experientially that there can be meaning even when I could not *do* anything.

"For many months when I tried to be useful I grew discouraged. Prior to my illness, I had always been able to do anything I set my mind on doing. In addition, I had always evaluated my days in terms of how much I had accomplished. Tangible production was my measure of usefulness, but now I couldn't produce. Furthermore, I couldn't judge my days by how I felt because my emotions were so often out of my control. As a recent bone marrow transplant patient, my accomplishments and my feelings were inappropriate standards for evaluating my day; I needed a new criterion.

"The amount of time I spent with God became my new criterion for judging how a day went, regardless of my lack of productivity or my unpleasant emotions. It seemed to be a relatively objective standard which called for actions and attitudes that were within my control. Lying on the sofa exhausted from vomiting, I could tell God how I felt. I could worship while listening to music. I could pray for others. I could comment to God about the TV show I was watching or the novel I was reading—no matter how 'useless' I felt by my 'normal' standards. When I had consciously spent time with God throughout the day, I could in all honesty say, 'It's been a good day!' even if I did lie on the sofa incapacitated the whole time. I grew to appreciate a statement Oswald Chambers makes in *Baffled to Fight Better*:

> It is not what a man *does* that is of final importance, but what he *is* in what he does. The atmosphere produced by a man, much more than his activities, has the lasting influence.[8]

"I discovered a great paradox: Often when we as Christians produce nothing physically, God can produce great spiritual treasures in ourselves and other people. I had to learn (and am still learning) to do all I can with my physical and mental capabilities, yet realize that these do not define the limits of my usefulness. The good produced in and through a person's life can reach as far and touch as deeply as God's Spirit can. I came to honestly agree with the apostle Paul that when I am so weak, I can see God's strength and the effects of His power all the more.[9]

God Works It All Together for Good

"I have seen God bring good out of my illness not only in my own life, but also in the lives of other people. My illness itself has been humbling, but so has the experience of seeing God change people's lives—through His power at work while I suffered, rather than through anything I myself did. Kurt is a good example. When I met him in the junior high group I didn't like him—he seemed angry. That's because he *was* angry. He had hardly ever been shown real love by his mother, who used drugs. However, during my illness he proved to be unusually sensitive and perceptive. After John and I were engaged and I was in the hospital, he watched John like a hawk, always asking, 'How's Susan?' He was sensitive enough to realize that John's exhaustion resulted more from emotional strain than a lack of sleep. Yet Kurt's eyes always seemed to be testing John, as if to say, 'I want to see if you'll stick by her!' He even seemed to be testing God with, 'You're not going to let her die, are You?'

"He questioned because he could not bear to see another betrayal after experiencing so much betrayal at home. Neither John nor God let him down. And Kurt is a much happier, more contented person today. I do not by any means claim that my illness is the whole reason his faith has grown; his father loves him deeply and John spent numerous hours in one-on-one time with him. Nevertheless, his watching John and God prove faithful during our pain has contributed to his growth.

"We often have a predetermined idea of how our lives are going to be and how God is going to use us. I had really been looking forward to my senior year of college with my hopes and plans of how God would use me that year. The leukemia shattered many of those expectations. But I have learned that we often don't know how God is going to use us. Later that year, some friends from college related to my mother how some of our conversations in the hospital had literally changed their lives.

"God influenced other people, too, in ways I would not have dreamed. One day not long after my first hospitalization, my mother received a call from a woman in our church. She had been upset for some time over a doctrinal difference of opinion within the church. My family had previously been labeled the 'old guard'— opponents of her view. She told my mother, 'Betty, I have to ask your forgiveness for all the anger I've had at you. And I must forgive you because I want to pray for Susan and can't until I forgive.' I pray for continued reconciliation between Christians from different perspectives as a result of my suffering and God's faithfulness.

"When the leaders of our church met to pray before I first went into the hospital, our pastor encouraged us to 'let this be an opportunity to draw together as a family.' It has been. My family has learned how to express emotions that we never felt free to before. Not only do we communicate more openly with each other, we are more vulnerable about our feelings and weaknesses with friends outside the family as well. As a result, we enjoy our time with both family and friends more, too.

"My father has his own list of ways he has seen God bring good out of our situation, which he tells himself:"

It was such a painful ordeal to see Susan suffer that it seemed impossible to hope that any good could come out of it. There were days that I didn't even want to consider the possibility of any "good result," "meaning," or "purpose" in this apparent catastrophe. Instead, my heart cried out, "God, You must be making a mistake!"

Nevertheless, I have seen myself change in several ways because of Susan's illness.

I have experienced the love and care of Christians like I never have before. I have been personally impressed with how temporal life is and how only the eternal values really count. As a result, I have a greater freedom in talking about my relationship with God. Especially with my non-Christian colleagues, I had been overly concerned about what they think of me and was afraid of offending them. These concerns fade after dealing with death.

I have a renewed sense that God does answer prayer. In the earlier years of my Christian life I saw some significant answers to prayer. In more recent times, though, I have struggled with doubts as to whether my prayers got any higher than the ceiling. During Susan's illness I would tell Him, "Lord, no matter what happens in our situation I will continue to believe in You and follow You. But I have to admit that if Susan isn't healed, I will have a hard time praying in the future. I'll have a hard time believing You will answer *my* prayers." Now, the fact that God intervened in such a significant way has strengthened my belief not only that He is there, but that He also answers prayer.

Finally, God has given me a deep internal desire to praise and worship Him. Before Susan's illness I often praised and worshiped God out of obedience. During the darkest valleys when she was suffering so much and her death seemed so certain, it seemed impossible to be joyful or thankful in the situation, despite the biblical injunctions to do so.[10] But I was accepting God's will in the matter and, to my surprise, I found welling up from deep within my heart a genuine desire to praise and worship God. This was a new experience for me. With joy I can tell you that it continues.

Throughout Susan's illness, many people cared for our family and prayed for us. Sunday school classes prayed for her regularly and little children reminded their parents to pray for her at bedtime. God demonstrated His love to us through the prayers and kindness of our church. He, in turn, demonstrated His faithfulness to them through us. I think of a comment that several people have made to Susan: "You're a walking inspiration. Just seeing you at church, alive and doing well, strengthens my faith when I go through difficulties. Praise God!"

"To What End?"

"One evening, while walking around the fourth floor with my ever-present IV pump, I [Susan] stopped to gaze out of a large plate-glass window at the lights of Los Angeles. I found myself trying to grasp the concept of millions of suffering people in the world. I mused, 'Here I am in a huge 700-bed hospital, and it's just one of hundreds of hospitals in one city! And the people here are the 'lucky' ones—here they can treat illnesses that would definitely be fatal for people in so many other countries!'

"Looking out that window, trying to see past the lights of the city to the suffering world beyond, I realized that the feeling of randomness and purposelessness behind it all was what really troubled me. I felt that I would prefer to suffer from overt persecution because I was a Christian—at least the suffering would have meaning then. I knew God was in control; I wanted to believe He had a purpose for my suffering. But in the midst of it all, no plan was apparent. The leukemia seemed to be inflicted by chance, to have no relation to my faith. Was I only a pawn in the battle between God and Satan, a casualty in the cosmic struggle between good and evil?"

This book started out asking the proverbial "Why?"— "Why did this happen to me?" "Why did this happen to my daughter?" "Why is there suffering in the world?"—

often a person's first response to suffering. So Susan and I have tried to provide as accurate an answer as we can give. But in the final analysis, "Why?" is really the wrong question. Helmut Thielicke said, when preaching during air raids in Germany during World War II, that in asking "Why?" there is often an implied criticism of God. He goes on to say that this stems from the notion that we know how God ought to act, and from a tendency to be immersed in ourselves. He comes to the conclusion that the question should not be "Why?" but "To what end?"[11]

Frankl and other philosophers often speak of "fate," defined as the "inevitable and often adverse outcome." It is true that the destructive forces of sin, evil men, and Satan have a tremendous influence over the world and cause good people to suffer. Yet humanity is not doomed or controlled by "fate." God is at work limiting the destructive forces. Periodically I had to remind myself of the fact that God is still in control and working to redeem any catastrophe; the forces of nature, sickness, self-centered men, or even Satan can operate only within the limits God establishes. Another sufferer put it this way:

> First, we must recognize with absolute certainty that God is in control in His universe. He is sovereign over evil, sin, death. Though for His own inscrutable reasons God has allowed Satan certain temporary powers, the Evil One holds them only under God's sovereignty. Satan's powers may be great, but they are limited both in intensity and in duration. So far may he go in his wicked intent against God's people, but no farther. He may hurt us, but he cannot ultimately harm us. The ultimate triumph is God's and ours in Him.[12]

During Susan's illness, the confidence that God remained in control and would use the situation for good and for His glory helped me find meaning in my own suffering. I looked to the Old Testament patriarch Joseph as an example. Years after they sold him into slavery, he told his cruel brothers, "You intended to harm me, but God intended it for good to accomplish what is now being done, the saving of many lives."[13]

One of the most common verses quoted on the subject of suffering, Romans 8:28, states, "God causes all things to work together for good to those who love God, to those who are called according to His purpose." I had to remind myself, though, that this promise has a condition: "to those who love God and are called according to His purpose." It's up to us to cooperate with God in order for His purposes to be achieved. Ultimately, each individual determines whether his suffering will be used for God's glory or whether it will be wasted. Suffering is painful and difficult—but wasted suffering is even worse.

The choice to make our suffering glorify God is the natural extension of the choice to make our life glorify God. The honor of being on earth to glorify God remains *the* worthy purpose, regardless of our circumstances. The deepest meaning—that which has eternal value— transcends questions of happiness and suffering. Viktor Frankl pondered this truth. When it seemed he would die, his concern was different than that of his comrades:

> Their question was, "Will we survive the camp? For, if not, all this suffering has no meaning." The question which beset me was, "Has all this suffering, this dying around us, a meaning? For, if not, then ultimately there is no meaning to survival; for a life whose meaning depends upon such a happenstance—

whether one escapes or not—ultimately would not be worth living at all."[14]

Often Susan thought about and wrote journal entries on this issue of finding a reason to live regardless of whether or not she was healed. Here are her conclusions:

"Early in my illness, I kept thinking: *'I don't want to be dead in five years!'* Later I modified my plea, *'Let me live—for John, Lord—let me live.'* These were gut-level, all-consuming pleas that pounded through me. Then one day, as I wrestled with and prayed through my feelings, a new realization completely replaced those appeals. Instead of turmoil, I felt a calm as it dawned on me, 'I can't live for John; I can only live for God.' The following month, after getting out of the hospital, I inscribed:

> I'm resolving something: Whenever I'm reminded of my leukemia (cleaning the Hickman, just noticing it, taking my pills, recalling my lack of hair, etc.) I'll ask our God and Father to give me a pure-hearted desire to live for Him. . . . Life is meaningless apart from the Lord. . . . I want a desire to live which grows out of God's Spirit within me and works to bring about His will on earth (as long as the greater good would come from my life rather than by my death). I want everything about my life to show gratitude; He gave His life for me. I want my desire to live—the desire itself—to be one which glorifies God; one which recognizes Him as absolute Lord, the Creator of the Universe, the source of all life.

Part V
Appendices

How to Help a Friend Who Is Hurting

EVERYBODY'S DIFFERENT

"One day in December 1987, I [Susan] cleaned my closet and discovered three nightgowns friends had made for me that had snaps down the front for a Hickman catheter. I don't intend to ever need the snaps for a Hickman again, but I wanted someone to enjoy the almost-new nightgowns, so I wrapped them up as presents and brought them with me to U.C.L.A. I asked for the names of three women with leukemia and went in to visit them. All three were in approximately the same physical condition, yet I was amazed at the radical difference in their attitudes.

"The first woman, Joanne, was in remission and was waiting for a bone marrow transplant. She was having a bad day—had been bored, cranky, and anxious all day. Yet, when I told her that I had had a bone marrow transplant, she exclaimed, 'I've never seen anyone who had a transplant and lived!' I could sympathize totally with her, knowing exactly how she felt. She cried and I hugged her. She told me how unfair she felt her situation was—she didn't deserve this—she had worked so hard to get off drugs and to establish her own business. She was mad at God—her business had just gotten to where she wanted it to be when 'God sent the leukemia,' as she put it. I told her those feelings were normal. She cried some more as I hugged her. I asked if she really wanted some answers to her whys. When she said she did, I briefly told her about the things we have explained in this book. Before long she was joking with her nurses, which I felt free to enter into, and we spent a thoroughly enjoyable hour together despite the pain we both felt. As I was leaving, amidst more tears and hugs, I left her with my phone number and I wrote on a poster of hers, 'Joanne: REMEMBER—IT WON'T LAST FOREVER. I love you and God loves you. Susan.'

"Next, I went to visit a woman who had had one round of chemotherapy, hadn't gotten a remission, and then had gone through a second round. She was waiting for her counts to come up to find out if she had gotten a remission. The anxiety of waiting was completely consuming her. I tried to encourage her by telling her she had survived this far; I had had a relapse and lived; another person I knew had lived even though he had gone through three rounds of chemotherapy without getting a remission. In short, I tried to give her reasons to hope. She reacted by saying, 'But not me—I feel like I'm not going to make it.' Her whole face wrinkled up in a teary whine. The room felt weighted down, oppressive. I couldn't help but think to myself, 'With that attitude she probably won't make it.' I felt like it was pointless trying to encourage her because she wouldn't let herself be encouraged. Yet I tried not to judge her—I don't know her background or struggles. A month in isolation waiting for the results of that bone marrow test does awful things to your emotions—emotions that you have little control of in that situation. I knew I had to try to encourage her, so I told her, 'You only have to get through one day at a time.' "

" 'But I want to live. I don't want to die!'

" 'Don't think about the future now. You can't do anything about the future now.'

" 'But I can't help it. I'm scared—I'm so scared.'

" 'Just get through today. Just six more hours. All you have to do is survive six more hours,' I said. 'That's all.'

" 'But it's so hard!'

" 'And tomorrow you just have to live through one more day—try to smile at someone, try and think of something hopeful. That's *all* you have to do!' "

" 'Yes, but it's so hard—I'm so scared!'

"And so it went: It's difficult to empathize with someone with such a grim prognosis and yet give a few rays of hope.

"She did appreciate the nightgown, although she could hardly believe a stranger would bring her a gift. I read her some psalms that spoke about God's understanding and compassion and said goodbye, my heart heavy as I left the room.

"Across the hall was the third woman I visited. She had just been given some medication and was asleep. The nurse gently woke her. I left the gift, told her I was a former leukemia patient, and gave her a hug. She smiled sleepily, thanked me warmly, and I left so she could go back to sleep."

As Susan's day at the hospital illustrates, there can't be a prepackaged formula that you give when visiting a suffering friend. There is no foolproof "right thing to say." Recognize that what you say will be different for each person because every person's circumstances and personality are unique.

Romans 12:15 tells us to "Rejoice with those who rejoice, and weep with those who weep." The Book of Ecclesiastes says: "There is a time for everything, and a season for every activity under heaven."[1] There is a time to talk, a time to simply be with the person; a time to give answers and explanations, a time to just listen; a time to visit, a time to give the person time alone. We need to keep in mind the wisdom of the Book of Proverbs: "Like apples of gold in settings of silver is a word spoken in right circumstances."[2]

Throughout the gospels, Christ ministered to people

according to their individual needs. For example, when Lazarus died, Jesus ministered to his sisters in different ways. Martha seemed to be trying to understand why her brother died, so Jesus explained the resurrection of the dead to her. But with Mary, who fell weeping at His feet, Jesus simply wept.[3]

Keep in Mind the Stages of Suffering

Remembering the emotional stages that people go through when they suffer can often give clues on how to best help them. A person in the stage of denial and isolating himself may not want to see you. He may deny there is any illness or be convinced he is healed when all the evidence indicates otherwise. Try not to take the rejection personally and continue to express your love despite his resistance to you. Later on you may find that he has realized his need for your friendship, but may have difficulty asking for it. Be available to reestablish the friendship later.

The anger stage may manifest itself in many ways: in irritability, self-pity, criticism, or even outright rage or bitterness. The person in this stage is probably the hardest one to relate to as he often vents his feelings on those closest to him. Not only does he get angry at God, but also at the people who can potentially help him the most.

It is important to realize that with suffering and misfortune people often regress and become childlike—to a great extent, that's normal. Don't let it shock you. Be patient; try not to take your friend's outbursts or sarcasm personally. What your friend needs is someone who will accept him with his feelings so he can work through them. Let him know it is normal to feel like he does. Encourage him to express his feelings in prayer, by writing in a journal, or talking to a friend.

After Shawn Strannigan lost her son in an auto accident, she wrote in a magazine article, "The people I appreciated most were those who braved my anger. In my darker moments, I turned my wrath upon God and found that some were not able to deal with this." She recommends that friends "keep quiet during such storms, accept the bereaved person's anger, and resist the temptation to defend God. He can take care of Himself." She went on to say:

> I stayed furious with God for many months. On December 6, 1984, the day that would have been Jonah's fifth birthday, I did the unpardonable: I cursed God and waited miserably to die. Mercifully, I didn't, and that horrible day became a turning point in my grief process. When he didn't strike me dead, I began to realize how very much God loved me and how intimately he, who had lost his only son, understood my pain. I knew now that I would survive.[4]

When a person is feeling guilty and depressed, you may be able help relieve the guilt. Be careful, though, that you don't make his guilt worse, as some "encouragers" are known to do. One time when you visit, your friend may be full of hope, and you'll find that he is ministering to you instead of you to him. But a random event can bring all the negative feelings right back in an instant. Such mood shifts are normal.

One final note: A person may stay in a phase for months or years. Or these stages may merge with one another; or a person may go from one to the next and then back to an earlier stage. Don't expect your friend to progress in a neat, predictable manner. Be prepared for the unexpected when dealing with those who are in severe emotional pain.

PREPARING FOR THE VISIT

Know Why You Are Visiting

Before you go to visit someone, you need to ask yourself why you are visiting. Is it to alleviate your own guilt? Is it because the person is a relative and you ought to visit him? Is it because the person asked you to visit, but you really don't want to? Is it because you believe you have the right formula to solve his problem? In other words, do you want to visit this person out of your own need or agenda, or because you really care about the person? Hopefully, it is because you care and want to express this to your friend.

It's Okay to Feel Uncomfortable

Don't be surprised if you feel uncomfortable when you visit. Maybe you will have to say, "I just want to let you know that I feel kind of uncomfortable. I don't know what you need—I don't know how you feel. But I want you to know I care about you. Please tell me what I can do to help you and I'll try to do it." A great deal of our discomfort stems from the fact that when other people are suffering, it stirs up an awareness of our own vulnerability and mortality, at either a conscious or unconscious level. We need to be aware of our own feelings and anxieties as we try to comfort someone, and we need to be honest about them.

Be Prepared for What You Will See

Another wise course of action before going to visit someone who is seriously ill is to find out his condition. It is an art to appropriately prepare someone to see his loved one when tragedy has altered his appearance. *Tested by Fire* tells the story of Merrill Womach, who was severely burned in an airplane crash. The physician in charge told his wife: "I want you to know that your husband will not look quite like himself. He has been slightly burned." That was a gross understatement. She had to quickly excuse herself—lest she faint in his presence.[5]

For the first weeks after her accident, quadriplegic Joni Eareckson-Tada was strapped into a Stryker frame with metal tongs in her skull for traction. Two friends came to visit, took one look, and rushed to the hall and vomited—not what you would call an encouraging visit.[6]

Help Bridge the Isolation Gap

Another cause of our discomfort when visiting people is the physical surroundings of the hospital. Not only do they make visitors uncomfortable, but they even separate the person emotionally from other people, adding to his feelings of isolation. In a hospital room, most visitors feel very out-of-place. Their friend is lying in a giant bed guarded by trays, tubes, sandbags, and pillows, while the visitors perch gingerly on plastic chairs wondering, "What do all those machines *do*?" The visitor usually vacillates between thinking, "He probably needs to talk about what he's going through," and "He must have told a hundred people how he's doing—I don't want to bother him by asking him again!" The best thing to do is just ask if he wants to tell you about his illness or not. Then make sure you take him at his word. We invest the paraphernalia and the awkwardness of hospital visits with greater power to isolate when we fail to talk about them. Be straightforward about your discomfort. Don't be afraid to ask about the gadgets or his daily schedule. Give him the opportunity to let you into his world.

Find Out the Need

Another thing you can do to prepare for a visit is find out from relatives, close friends, or nurses how your friend is doing physically and emotionally. What is his greatest need at this time? Is it a good time for you to visit? Often you can best help the person who is in pain or sedated by making your visit brief. Sometimes it may be appropriate to bring something you can do and just sit and keep him company. If the person is mentally alert, reading a psalm or something of interest may be appreciated. Is their greatest problem loneliness or boredom? Then a simple game might be appropriate or a cassette or video tape appreciated. For some, a humorous poster or card can be "just what the doctor ordered."

YOUR VISIT

What *Not* to Say

Linda Sarner is a family therapist whose two-year-old son was killed when hit by a car. As a result of this tragedy, she decided to study the ways people respond to the grief-stricken. The following is an excerpt from an article written about her:

> "I'm not sure that everyone knows that there isn't anything they can say to make it [the loss] better," Sarner says. "We still hear people trying and trying to come up with the right thing to say to bereaved parents to take their pain away."
>
> One of the most common, and most wounding, remarks is, "You're young. You can still have more children."
>
> "What a bereaved parent hears with that is the implication, 'My son is replaceable.' But he wasn't replaceable; he was one of a kind," Sarner says.

> Another try at consolation is the statement,
> "He's better off. If he'd lived, he would have
> been a vegetable."[7]

Saying to someone who is hurting, "Things could be worse" implies that they do not really have any reason to feel like they do. It makes light of their pain. Other remarks that tend to alienate the person instead of comfort them are "It was God's will" and "It was for the best" or "Time will heal." All of these remarks have one thing in common: They stifle or even deny a person the right to his feelings.

One of the greatest injustices we do to people who are in the midst of suffering is to rob them of their feelings. The most obvious example of this is when someone tells another person that they should not feel worried, depressed, angry, etc. However, there are more subtle forms such as: "Look on the bright side," "Count your blessings," "God knows what He's doing," "Praise God anyway," "Be glad for the victory we have in Christ," "There must be a reason behind this," and "All things work together for good." All of these have truth in them, but when they are said at the wrong time, they convey the message that feelings of anger, depression, of being isolated from others and from God are wrong or even sinful.

Another great injustice we can do to those who are suffering is to lay a guilt trip on them. A patient of mine, whose son committed suicide, was told: "He [the son] was waiting for you to get home, maybe." What a guilt inducer! Other comments given to the father suggested that the "encouragers" were more concerned with themselves than with the grieving father. Such statements as "I pray that my child will be safe" or "Thank God we got help for ours in time" reveal how insensitive "comforters" can be to the pain of the sufferer.

So What *Can* You Say?

As deeply as you may hurt with and grieve for your suffering friend, you still can never really understand what he is feeling. Susan remembers that when visitors said things to her like, "I can sort of relate to what you're going through—I had this terrible bout of flu last year," she would think to herself, "You have no idea what you're talking about." Incidents like that made her withdraw from that person and sometimes from other people as well. Proverbs says, "Only the person involved can know his own bitterness or joy—no one else can really share it."[8] Only God can say, "I know just how you feel." But friends *can* express their love without claiming to understand or relate. Article after article written on this topic assert that generally the best thing you can say is a simple and sincere "I'm sorry," accompanied by a hug, holding a hand, or some kind of gentle touch.

If you really have had a similar experience, do share it. Be careful not to sound as if you are trying to "outdo" the other person with tales of suffering or giving an instant prescription based on how you handled your situation. Instead, seek to strengthen your bond with your friend in order to bridge the isolation gap that so often develops between the sufferer and the rest of the world. Let your vulnerability with your own feelings give him permission to be open about what he is experiencing.

Do say what you feel—with sensitivity and awareness as to how it will be perceived. The book *The Healer's Art* makes this comment:

> People make small talk in the presence of big problems, [not because] they don't want to talk about the important issues, but [because] they don't know how. Often the family or even physicians are afraid of saying "the wrong

thing," so they say nothing. The patient takes the cue and the silence goes on—and so does the loneliness.[9]

Keep an open door to communication through which your friend can enter, if he wants to.

Be Wary of Overoptimism

The importance of a sense of humor and of being hopeful cannot be overemphasized. But again there is a time to lighten the mood with humor and a time to cry with the person. Viktor Frankl commented that "it was the incorrigible optimists who were the most irritating companions."[10] Proverbs says, "Being happy-go-lucky around a person whose heart is heavy is as bad as stealing his jacket in cold weather, or rubbing salt in his wounds."[11]

Studies have shown that an overly optimistic person who is trying to help someone who feels hopeless can actually make the person feel worse.[12] Once Betty shared her fears with a friend during a crisis point in Susan's illness, only to be told, "You've got to be positive. There's a lot of healing in being positive." Looking back on the incident, she says that though the statement was true, "It was absolutely no comfort at all; in fact it made me angry and I was able to level with her as to the facts that we were dealing with. Then this person realized that she didn't know the facts and what we were facing." People can hurt each other without even realizing it.

When to Confront

"In much wisdom there is much grief, and increasing knowledge results in increasing pain."[13] Sometimes as a well-meaning visitor, you may feel the need to help the sufferer "face reality" if he is in a denial phase of his illness. But be careful. Some hospitalized cardiac patients who did not want to talk about their illness—seemingly "not facing reality"—did worse when information was forced on them. Similarly, when some parents of children with leukemia were confronted with the facts of the situation, they went through much more physical and psychological stress.[14] A certain amount of denial—at the right time—can actually be useful for the patient. However, if a person's denial prevents him from receiving crucial treatment, such as the heart patient with severe chest pain, an individual with symptoms highly suggestive of cancer, or a diabetic not taking his medication, such behavior may warrant confrontation. However, someone who is receiving treatment or whose situation cannot be altered should not be forced to "face the facts" against his wishes.

Occasionally your friend may get stuck in a negative phase of his grief. It may become useful to confront him in a loving manner, especially if he is alienating other people. However, try to do your confronting when both of you are in a relatively good mood. Express your feelings with statements such as, "I know this hospitalization must be very difficult for you, making you want to scream at everybody. I can understand that, but it hurts me when you yell at me. Let's work this out." Kind confrontation may prove to be extremely beneficial for all parties involved.

The Process Takes Time

Accept the fact that a sufferer has to walk through the valley of the shadow of his own feelings, and that the journey often takes time. The grieving process after the death of a loved one usually takes six to 24 months. Losing a mate has been compared to having a leg amputated—even when it has healed, there is still the constant reminder of the loss. An outside person trying to hurry the process along typically makes things worse, forcing the bereaved to bury his feelings rather than work through them.

Often the most difficult times surface long after the initial tragedy. It is not uncommon for families who have lost a loved one to hit their deepest lows when their ordeal "is over." It's easy for people to think they are getting on with their lives when in reality they may be struggling more than ever. Continue to reach out to these families. They need your cards and letters for many months. Extra support during "special days" such as birthdays, holidays, and the anniversary of the deceased can bring them special comfort.

THE SUPPORT SYSTEM

Tangible Support

When comforting those who are suffering, it is important to minister to their physical needs as well as their spiritual and emotional needs. Take the initiative in doing or offering to do things for those going through suffering. Sometimes the bereaved are unaware of their own needs, so be alert to those which are unspoken. They may be too timid to ask for help. No matter how much you mean it, just saying "Let me know if I can do something for you" usually does not suffice.

The sufferer doesn't know how willing you really are and so may be reluctant to ask for help, especially if his needs seem to be mundane. If they need a ride to the hospital, house repairs, the lawn mowed—do they dare ask you to help with things like that? It is far better for you to be specific in your offer for help: "Let me know if I can do anything for you. I'd be glad to give you a ride to the hospital, do yard work, help with your taxes—just let me know how I can help." We had people keep us company on the long ride to the hospital, drive Susan to the hospital for her follow-up visits, bring food to the

family, and even clean our house and yard—all of which
were accepted and greatly appreciated.

A Word of Caution to the Family

It is also crucial that you consider the effect the ill
person has on your entire family. An ill child tremendously affects both the parents' marriage and the other
children. Sometimes in people's concern for the ill person, the family gets lost in the shuffle. This is especially
devastating in prolonged illnesses. As parents of a sick
child or as the spouse of someone who is ill, it is very
important that you as a couple are able to relate openly
with each other, to solve problems and disagreements,
to keep your priorities straight relative to time, money,
and energy. You will need to be aware of the emotional
stresses, needs, and adjustments of your spouse and
other children, helping those who are well to cope with
their own everyday feelings and problems without their
feeling cheated of the time and energy being given to
the sick person.

Be realistic about the stress upon yourself as a support
person and look for a friend who will listen to you.
Especially if you are a family member constantly caring
for an ill or grieving relative, schedule outdoor time,
private time, and occasional activities you really enjoy.
Accept God's comfort for yourself—draw strength from
Him—and leave the ultimate responsibility for your
spouse's, child's, or parent's well-being in His hands.

Specialized Support

As you try to support your friend or relative, you may
be tempted to think you are not being much help. On
the contrary, support systems have an undisputed positive effect. One study showed that the presence of a
supportive laywoman who sat with women in labor

shortened the delivery time, increased the likelihood of the mother's being awake after delivery and being involved with her infant, and decreased the complications.[15] One researcher called a support system a "buffer against stressful life events."[16] Such social support systems provide intimacy, a sense of well-being, nurture, the reassurance of self-worth, assistance, guidance, and advice, as well as access to contacts and information. It has been determined that those who are single, separated, widowed, or divorced have much higher mortality rates, regardless of their illness.[17]

Friends and family, even if they are Christians, cannot always meet all of a person's needs, though. He may need to seek professional help or people who have personally experienced the same kind of suffering. Support groups for cancer victims and their families, Alcoholics Anonymous, Al-Anon, and similar organizations can provide informed and empathic aid. Try to find hospital forums that give professional lectures, along with discussion time. The American Cancer Society, hospitals, and churches can help you in locating support groups. However, beware of groups where everyone merely airs their grievances and commiserates together. (Further suggestions for support groups are given in chapter 13 of the application section.)

The Support of Your Presence

> A little girl came home from visiting a neighbor whose young daughter had died recently.
> "Why did you go?" questioned the father.
> "To comfort the mother," said the child.
> "What could you do to comfort her?" asked the father.
> "I climbed in her lap and cried with her," said the child.[18]

There will be times when just being *with* the other person is more important than anything you can say or do. The custom in some parts of Africa is that when someone has died, friends come over and simply sit with the family, grieving in silence. Joseph Bayly, who has had three sons die, describes a similar experience in his book *The Last Thing We Talk About*:

> I was sitting, torn by grief. Someone came and talked to me of God's dealings, of why it happened, of hope beyond the grave. He talked constantly, he said things I knew were true.
>
> I was unmoved, except to wish he'd go away. He finally did.
>
> Another came and sat beside me. He didn't talk. He didn't ask leading questions. He just sat beside me for an hour and more, listened when I said something, answered briefly, prayed simply, left.
>
> I was moved. I was comforted. I hated to see him go.[19]

You don't have to have all the answers. Your prayerful presence can work wonders. Remember that God ultimately is the source of all wisdom, healing, and wholeness. Oswald Chambers wrote the following: "The biggest benediction one man can find in another is not in his words, but that he implies: 'I do not know the answer to your problem, all I can say is that God alone must know; let us go to Him.' "[20]

Applying Healing Principles

Compiled by Betty Carlson

Individuals reading this manuscript have asked for some direction in applying the healing principles described in it. The following questions are designed to assist you. It also may help you to clarify your thoughts and feelings by writing them down or expressing them to a friend.

Chapters 7 and 8—God's Purpose in Suffering and Promises to Hold Onto

1. Isaiah 55:8,9 says that God's ways are far higher than ours.
   a. Read this passage and tell God your reaction.
   b. Do you agree that our view of suffering may well be very limited as compared to God's viewpoint?
   c. To what extent has this book given you new insights, and what remains unanswered for you?

2. Are you prone to take life, health, and loved ones for granted? Think of ways you can change in this regard.

3. Is God trying to get your attention? If so, what might He be trying to say to you?

4. As stated in chapter 7, suffering is the result of the sin of mankind which has separated us from God, but God has provided a means of reconciliation. Have you experienced His reconciliation through Christ and do you have an eternal hope?
   If not, the following Bible verses might be helpful: (For those of you who are unfamiliar with the Bible: First

of all, the 66 books in the Bible are listed in the Table of Contents in the front of each Bible. Second, for ease in locating a reference, each book is divided into chapters and verses. For example, John 3:16 means that the reference is found in the book of John, chapter 3 and verse 16.)

    a. If you want to be reconciled with God, study the following verses: John 3:16; John 1:12,13; Romans 6:23. Also, you might find these books helpful:

       Billy Graham, *Peace with God*, Word Publishing Company, 1984.

       C.S. Lewis, *Mere Christianity*, Macmillan Company, 1952.

       John R. Stott, *Basic Christianity*, InterVarsity Press, 1972.

    b. Regarding your responsibility in your illness:

       1) As this book has described, there is a great tendency to inappropriately blame the sufferer for his illness. Are you being inappropriately blamed by others or by yourself? If false guilt is the cause, refuse to accept it. If you are unsure, discuss it with a trusted friend or counselor.

       2) If on the other hand you believe your inappropriate actions or sin have caused your illness, the following passages tell how you can receive God's promise of forgiveness and acceptance regardless of what you have done: Psalm 32:5; 1 John 1:9; Romans 8:1.

       3) Once you have worked through 1) and 2) above, do not allow yourself or other people to flagellate you. Go on—that's what God would have you do.

    c. Carefully review the seven assurances given in chapter 8, pages 90-92. For those assurances which you do not feel sure of, you might find the verses and comments in the Notes for chapter 8 helpful.

5. Review "Seven of God's Redemptive Uses of Suffering" on pages 84-87. Which is the most applicable to your situation? Why? Chapter 17 elaborates on this topic.

6. To what degree has your love for God or trust in Him been tested? If you are having difficulty in this area:
   a. Might 1 Corinthians 10:13 be applicable?
   b. Tell God exactly how you are struggling, and/or
   c. Discuss this with an understanding Christian or pastor.

7. Think about the fact that there is no inward growth without pain of some kind.
   a. How do you respond to this?
   b. Though you may not know what God is doing now, can you trust that He is purifying your life in order to develop Christian character? List the areas in which He might be working.

8. Enumerate ways in which your suffering is or could enable you to be more sensitive to other people.
   a. Brainstorm on all the possible ways you might be of help to other people because of your situation.
   b. Pray for God's guidance as you pursue any of these avenues.

9. Are you willing to let God be glorified through your present circumstance? In other words, can you say "Not my will, but Thine, be done?" If not, what changes might you need to make in yourself in order to do so?

(If you are interested in further study of these questions, the Notes have more Bible verses on many of these issues.)

Chapter 10—Face Your Feelings

1. To help you get in touch with your *feelings*:
   a. Take out a piece of paper and as you think about your situation, just start writing whatever comes

to mind. Among your thoughts, feelings will come to you.

b. If you don't know where to begin, review the stages starting on page 113: denial, anger, bargaining, depression, anxiety, guilt, acceptance, or any others you may be feeling, and list them on your paper, leaving room to write your feelings.

c. Start writing whatever comes to mind about any of the above feelings no matter how slight or insignificant it may seem. For example, you may not get angry but may be aware of many "small irritations." You may not think you are depressed, but find yourself crying more than you usually do. You may not be aware of denial but notice your procrastination in following your doctor's orders.

d. It's important to suspend any judgment about the appropriateness of your feelings—just list what you feel.

e. In the future, continue to ask yourself, "What am I feeling now?" Add any additional feelings to this sheet and/or clarify those you already have listed.

2. Now deal with your *thoughts*:

a. Write out whatever thoughts you are having about your situation. Be as specific as possible.

b. For each thought, write out the logical feelings that follow such a thought. For example, one patient told himself, "I'll never be happy again." The resultant feelings were deep depression. Another patient told herself, "I'll never be well again" and felt hopeless. Your thoughts play an important role in affecting your feelings.

3. In order to begin to get past these negative thoughts and feelings, you will need to "own" them. That is, to accept them as your own without any self-condemnation for having them.

4. If you have some thoughts that make your situation worse, work on replacing them with helpful thoughts. For example: Instead of telling yourself, "I'll never be well again," tell yourself, "With God's help, there will be some good days ahead."

5. Now share these thoughts and feelings:
   a. Pray that you will be able to share at least some of these thoughts and feelings with a trusted friend or relative.
   b. You may need to mentally rehearse your opening, "You know, Sue, you're my closest friend, and I appreciate all your help during my troubles. I've been carrying a number of negative feelings all by myself. They're weighing me down and I need to share them with someone. Would you mind if I shared them with you? I'm fearful you might be offended or think less of me. But if you could suspend any judgments and just listen to me, it would be so helpful."
   c. If there is no one with whom you can talk openly, seriously consider finding a minister, counselor, or support group you can talk with.

6. A number of months after Susan's transplant I needed to be honest with my feelings toward God. I started a letter to Him as follows: "Dear God, You know the truth that in recent months I have been mad at You, blaming You for the fact that things haven't gone the way I wanted. The things I am referring to are..." Do you need to write such a letter to God?

Chapter 11—Seek Appropriate Help

1. Seek God's help:
   a. Both in your private prayers and with some trusted friends, prayerfully seek God's direction and assistance for your present situation.

b. Consider asking some church leaders, a care group, or "prayer chain" to pray for God's healing and direction in your life.

2. Seek medical help:
   a. Have you sought the best medical assistance available?
   b. Do you have questions or qualms about your diagnosis or treatment?
   c. Is there some unusual or difficult aspect of your illness that would make a second opinion or consultation with another physician or a specialist appropriate?
   d. If indicated, pursue further medical help. If you know someone in the medical field—a doctor or a nurse—and trust his judgment, he is your best source for medical referrals. Otherwise, a knowledgeable friend or acquaintance whom you trust can be helpful.

Chapter 12—The Will to Health

If you are feeling that you have no control in your present situation and you don't know where to start:

1. Prayerfully consider if there are any areas where you can gain at least a measure of control.

2. In a column on the left side of a piece of paper, list everything that is included in your daily routine. Be sure to include the little, everyday activities often taken for granted.

3. Now make three smaller columns to the right and label as follows:
   a. Activities out of my control.
   b. Activities over which I now am exercising control.
   c. Activities in which I possibly could exercise control.

Then mark with an X or write comments about each activity in the appropriate column. For example:

Daily Activities	Out of My Control	I Am Controlling	Possibly a Choice for Me
1. Sleep in	Sometimes I need to		At times I'm lazy
2. Breakfast		X	
3. Brush teeth		X	
4. Watch TV		X	
5. Therapy	X		
6. Plan meals			X
7. Read			X

4. Congratulate yourself for the choices you are already making (the middle column).

5. Choose the easiest area or two in the last column which you can, with God's help, begin to control.

6. As you are able, continue to add to the areas in which you are making choices for yourself.

Chapter 13—We Really Need Each Other

Is there sufficient social involvement in your life? Do you have individuals with whom you can share your innermost thoughts and feelings? If not, list some ways you can begin to enlarge this area of your life. Below are some ideas that may help.

1. Do you have a friend or acquaintance you would like to get to know better?
    a. You may need to pray and search for this person because:
        1) It may not be the person you first think it will be.

2) Until you find someone dependable and understanding, be open to people you may not know very well now.
   b. Set up a time to meet in an environment that will be conducive for conversation.
   c. Begin "sounding out" the possibility of meeting regularly to nurture a supportive relationship.
   d. Be sure that you are willing to be a supportive listener to him/her when he/she needs it and you are able.

2. If you are married, consider ways that you can enhance that relationship:
   a. Go on dates.
   b. Develop new interests together.
   c. Restore some of those interests you enjoyed when first dating.

3. If you are not already doing so, commit yourself to a group of caring people, such as a small fellowship within a church or other support group.

4. Find out about specialized support groups designed for people with your particular difficulty by:
   a. Calling your local hospital, clinic, or church.
   b. In some cities, you can call Information or consult your phone book under such headings as Community Services or Medical Support Groups.
   c. The appendix in Robert Veninga's book *A Gift of Hope* (Ballantine Books, 1987) gives a detailed list of specialized support groups.

Chapter 14—To Accept the Things I Cannot Change

1. In chapter 12 we dealt mainly with our control over our daily activities. Here we want to apply these principles not only to activities but to our attitudes as well. Pray that God will give you the wisdom to know the difference between the things you cannot change and

those which you can. Pray also for the courage to change what you can and to accept your "givens."

   a. Divide a piece of paper into three columns. On the left side, list your current problems. (Large ones may need to be broken down into various components.)

   b. In a second column, note the problems you cannot change and need to accept.

   c. In the third column, note the areas in which you can make changes.

For example:

The Problem	To Accept	To Change
Low energy level	My limitation that I can work only 4 hrs./day	Using my limited energy wisely
Unable to drive	The time it takes to get places, or to allow other people to take me.	Let my needs be known to appropriate persons. Walk when feasible. Be willing to take a bus or taxi.

2. Forgiveness:

In chapter 10 I shared part of a letter I had written to God. I concluded that letter with: " . . . Lord, forgive me for my anger at You, my resentment that things haven't gone the way I wanted. Help me to want to accept Your will in my life. Help me to see the many blessings You have given. Dwight."

   a. Consider whether or not you need to forgive someone: a relative, friend, doctor, or God.

   b. Clarify the specific hurt—don't tell yourself it didn't hurt or pretend it didn't happen.

   c. If you need to forgive someone you are still in contact with, decide whether or not you need to discuss it with that person. This discussion might be necessary for three different reasons:

      1) So that you *can* forgive the offender.

      2) For the offender's benefit.

      3) For the benefit of the relationship.

   d. Write out your intent to give up your anger or resentment and choose not to hold it against the person or God.

Chapter 15—The Healing Power of Hope

1. Is your glass half-empty?

   List your hopes or dreams that have been dashed. These may include items listed under "problems" in the application section of chapter 14.

2. Is your glass half-full?

   a. List your many blessings, past and present.

   b. What do you have that others may not have? Often we compare ourselves with those people who have so much more than we do. This can create problems for us in our thinking and feelings. To help keep this in balance:

      1) Make a list of several individuals you know who have *less* than you have.

      2) In what way does each person have less than you?

      3) In contrast, think about what you have that they do not have.

   c. Now list five general categories of people who have less than you have and then contrast it with what you have that is more. For example, you might list the bag lady who walks the streets of Los Angeles. She has no home, insufficient food, no family, and is cold. I have: a warm apartment, plenty of food, a caring family.

    d. Now thank God for any additional blessings that you have.

3. Consider how despair comes prior to hope:
   a. What do you think and feel about the thought, "True hope springs from despair"?
   b. From what or whom do you derive your hope?
   c. What is your temporal hope—what in this life are you yet hoping for?
   d. If you still need to find an eternal hope, do you know someone who seems to have such a hope?
   e. Consider talking with that person about it.
   f. Obtain a Bible and begin to read the Gospel of John, the Book of Romans, or Ephesians to see what it says about this issue. (You may also refer to the verses and books given in application #4, pages 199-200, or to the verses in the Notes for chapter 15.)

Chapter 16—Laughter, Praise, and Joy

1. Laughter:
   a. Think about the type of humor that makes you really laugh: e.g., certain comics, comedians, books, or films.
   b. Among your friends and acquaintances, list those with whom you can freely laugh the most. If being with them is uplifting, try and spend more time with them.
   c. Do you need to develop this area of your life? If so, begin in some way to make laughter a "regular activity." You might pick some situation, write out the details, or tell it to a good friend in the style you might use a year from now. Or you might imagine how it would be depicted on a television sit-com. See if you can get yourself to laugh at it. You may need to start with very minor incidents, but with practice, you can learn to laugh at many situations.

2. Praise and Thanksgiving:

Hebrews 13:15 (KJV) says "Let us offer the sacrifice of praise to God continually, that is, the fruit of our lips giving thanks to his name." Praise often is an act of obedience that at times may be difficult.

   a. Pick a psalm (such as 103 or 96-99) that expresses the grandeur of God. Think about it and try praising (or thanking) God for *who He is*.

   b. Recall the blessings listed in the previous exercise. Thank God for what He has done for you in the past and is doing now. "Most people do not give up on life because of a catastrophe. They give up because they *no longer see the small joys worthy of celebration.*"[1]

3. Joy:

It has been said that happiness depends on what happens to us, while Christian joy goes deeper and is independent of the circumstances. Are you looking for "happiness" or "joy"?

   a. Take some time to "smell the roses," to notice the splendor of a tree, or to listen to a bird sing the way you would if you had less-difficult circumstances.

   b. Go to a park, beach, or a scenic view and notice the nuances of color, texture, and sound.

   c. Ponder the greatness of God as Creator of all nature.

   d. Worship Him as you enjoy His creation.

Chapter 17—Suffering with Purpose and Meaning

1. Where do you think God is in your difficult situation?

   a. To what degree do you believe God knows and cares about you and your circumstances?

   b. To what degree do you believe God is bigger than your difficulty, working behind the scenes to bring good out of it?

   c. Consider memorizing Romans 8:28.

2. Your responsibility in finding meaning in your situation:

a. In order to find meaning in suffering a person has to move past the denial, anger, resentment, etc. Where are you in the process of accepting your difficulty and working toward meaning?

b. Are there any destructive thought patterns you need to consider changing regarding the purpose of your situation?

c. Think of several people you have heard of, read about, or know whom God has used despite or through their suffering. You may think of Joni, a quadriplegic; Merrill Womach, the singer burned in a plane crash; Fanny Crosby, the woman blinded as an infant who wrote thousands of great hymns and choruses; or people you know personally.

   1) Think of how meaningless their tragedy must have felt to them at the time.

   2) Now think of all the good results that God has brought from their lives.

d. Given the aspects of your situation that you cannot change, if the sky were the limit, what are all the conceivable ways God might infuse your life and situation with meaning? List them.

e. Think of persons to whom you can reach out. Now list specific ways you can reach out to them in a meaningful way.

Notes

Preface

1. As quoted by Edwin Young in *The Purpose of Suffering* (Eugene, OR: Harvest House Publishers, 1985), Preface.
2. O. Hallesby, Ph.D., *The Christian Life* (Minneapolis: Augsburg Publishing House, 1965), p. 112.
3. Helmut Thielicke, *Out of the Depths* (Grand Rapids, MI: William B. Eerdmans Publishing Company, 1962), Jacket.

Chapter 2—Life's Not Fair!

1. Teresa Simons, "Letters of Support Pour into Families of Victims," *News-Pilot*, December 19, 1984, p. A-1.
2. Scott Kraft, "Toll Threatens Hard-Earned Gains in Nations With Meager Resources," *Los Angeles Times*, August 9, 1987, Special Supplement, "AIDS, A Global Assessment," p. 3.
3. Viktor Frankl, *Man's Search for Meaning* (New York: Washington Square Press, 1959), pp. 69-70.
4. As reported in the 1973 *Los Angeles Times*, August 26, Part I; August 27, Part II; August 30, Part III.
5. Charles T. Powers, "Wesley Parker and the Will of God," *Los Angeles Times*, September 14, 1973, Part IV, p. 11.

Chapter 3—Who Is to Blame?

1. Job 1:8-12, TLB
2. Dr. Julius Segal, *Winning Life's Toughest Battles: Roots of Human Resilience* (New York: Ballantine Books, 1986), p. 5.
3. Eric J. Cassell, M.D., *The Healer's Art: A New Approach to the Doctor-Patient Relationship* (New York: Harper & Row, Inc., 1976), pp. 46, 129.
4. Thielicke, *Out of the Depths*, op. cit., pp. 10-11.
5. Job 1:16, NIV
6. The Bible sometimes records people's misunderstandings of God, even though inaccurate. However, by carefully reading the Scriptures this can be determined. An example is Job's messengers who suggested that God was responsible for the catastrophe Job faced. "The fire of God has fallen from heaven and burned up your sheep and all the herdsmen...." In addition, Job's wife said, "Are you still trying to be godly when God has done all this to you?" (Job 1:16; 2:9, TLB). In each instance the Bible merely records *their* conclusion, which was to blame God for the tragedy. Fortunately for us, God included the prelude—the first 13 verses of the first chapter which gives us the true interpretation of Job's suffering. Satan instigates; God allows.

7. Richard Critchfield, "World Masses May Grasp Progress If Put in Their Terms," *Los Angeles Times*, September 14, 1975, Part IX, p. 1.

8. "Indians Take Grave View of Volcanic Rumblings," *Los Angeles Times*, March 30, 1980.

9. Dan Williams, "Homeless Feel Ire Rising in Quake's Wake," *Los Angeles Times*, October 12, 1985, Part I, p. 1.

10. Segal, *Winning Life's Toughest Battles*, op. cit., p. 86.

11. Job 4:7; 5:8, TLB

12. John 9:2,3, NIV

13. Eugenia Price, *No Pat Answers* (Grand Rapids: Zondervan, 1972), pp. 60-61.

14. Job 8:6, TLB

15. Deuteronomy 4:40; 1 Chronicles 28:8,9

16. Zick Rubin, Letitia Anne Peplau, "Who Believes in a Just World," *Reflections*, a Merck Sharp & Dohme Publication, 1977, No. 1, Vol. XII, pp. 1-26.

17. William Nottingham, "Counselor Understands Agony of AIDS Affliction," *Los Angeles Times*, August 4, 1986, Part II, p. 1.

18. Job 4:12-16; 5:8,17, TLB

19. Oswald Chambers, *Baffled to Fight Better* (London: Marshall, Morgan & Scott, Ltd., 1955), p. 54.

20. Larry Parker, *We Let Our Son Die; A Parent's Search for Truth* (Eugene, OR: Harvest House Publishers, 1980), pp. 162, 165.

21. Luke 22:42

22. See Job 21:7-34; Psalm 73; Ecclesiastes 7:15; 8:14; John 9:1-3; 2 Corinthians 4:8,9; Hebrews 11; 1 Peter 2:20.

23. Hebrews 11:35, TLB

Chapter 4—How Can a Loving and All-Powerful God Allow Suffering?

1. From the film *The Hiding Place* (Minneapolis, MN: World Wide Pictures, 1975).

2. Harold S. Kushner, *When Bad Things Happen to Good People* (New York: Avon, 1981), p. 134.

3. John 3:16

4. Kushner, *When Bad Things Happen to Good People*, op. cit., p. 37.

5. Hebrews 6:18; Isaiah 1:15; Psalm 145:17

6. Walter Martin, from his tape series *To Every Man an Answer*, "Evil and Human Suffering," Vision House, Inc. (Ventura, CA: Gospel Light Publishers, 1976).

7. R.C. Sproul, *Reason to Believe* (Copyright © 1981 by R.C. Sproul; Grand Rapids, MI: Lamplighter Books, 1982), pp. 122-123. Used by permission of Zondervan Publishing House.

8. For an elaboration of this, see C.S. Lewis, *The Problem of Pain*, (New York: MacMillan Company, 1961), Chapter II.

9. Job 2:6

10. As I see it, there are three categories of things that God cannot do. First of all, as stated in the text, He cannot do those things that are contrary to His nature. Second, He cannot do things that by definition are mutually exclusive. For instance, He cannot make a square triangle or a rock so big

that He cannot carry it. Neither can He force people to voluntarily love Him. Third, God cannot alter the inevitable consequences of choices He has previously made. For example, once God decided to make man with free choice and man chooses to sin, the penalty of that sin must be paid by someone to satisfy God's innate justice.

11. Chambers, *Baffled to Fight Better*, op. cit., pp. 28, 29.
12. Mark 14:55-61
13. 2 Samuel 6:6-11, TLB; 1 Chronicles 13:6-14
14. 1 Chronicles 15:1,2,13-15
15. Deuteronomy 12:31, TLB
16. A.W. Tozer says: "His sovereignty requires that He be absolutely free, which means simply that He must be free to do whatever He wills to do anywhere at any time to carry out His eternal purpose in every single detail without interference. Were He less than free He must be less than sovereign." A.W. Tozer, *The Knowledge of the Holy* (New York: Harper & Brothers, 1961), p. 115.
17. Isaiah 55:8,9
18. Another difficult concept to understand is that pain may have its benefits. Let me illustrate. If you had the choice of never again having any pain, would you accept it? Usually when I ask this question to a group, about 20 percent would choose never to have any pain. It is understandable that those suffering with chronic pain would welcome total freedom from pain; however, even they might regret it. With no feeling of pain, a person would burn his fingers, stub his toes, sprain his ankles, or have a ruptured appendix and never know it. We need pain for survival. It gives warning signals of vital importance. This is the reason leprosy patients destroy their limbs. Children born with the inability to feel pain seldom live very long because their lives are in constant jeopardy. Dr. Macdonald Critchley, "Congenital Indifference to Pain," *Annals of Internal Medicine*, November 1956, Vol. 45, No. 5, pp. 737-747.
19. C.S. Lewis, *A Grief Observed* (New York: Bantam Books, 1976), p. 53.
20. Matthew 27:46
21. James 4:14, KJV; see also 1 Chronicles 29:15; Hebrews 11:24,25.
22. Joseph Heller, *Catch-22* (New York: Dell Publishing Company, Inc., 1961), pp. 184-185.
23. Kushner, *When Bad Things Happen to Good People*, op. cit., p. 129.
24. Lewis, *The Problem of Pain*, op. cit., p. 36.
25. Isaiah 45:9,10, TLB
26. Tozer, *The Knowledge of the Holy*, op. cit., pp. 36-37.

Chapter 5—God's Will and Suffering

1. Revelation 22:11,12
2. Genesis 1:31
3. Leslie D. Weatherhead, *The Will of God* (Nashville: Abingdon Press, 1944), chapter 2.
4. Romans 8:19-22
5. Matthew 19:8, TLB

6. Revelation 21:4
7. Genesis 4:4-8
8. Luke 13:2-5, TLB
9. Randolph J. Klassen, paper on "The Will of God," p. 3.
10. Ecclesiastes 7:15, TLB
11. Genesis 3:14-24
12. Tozer, *The Knowledge of the Holy*, op. cit., p. 110.
13. Genesis 3:17-19; Matthew 6:19,20. It is my opinion that moth and rust, thorns and thistles are a consequence of sin and therefore were not present in the garden nor will they be in heaven.
14. Editorials: Zinonas Danilevicius, M.D., "When Does CHD Start?" *Journal of American Medical Association*, December 11, 1974, Vol. 230, No. 11, pp. 1565-1566.
15. Sometimes people ask, "Why do animals suffer—they certainly haven't sinned." I believe that their suffering is also a result of man's original sin. Romans 8:19-23 (TLB) explains:

    > For all creation is waiting patiently and hopefully for that future day when God will resurrect his children. For on that day thorns and thistles, sin, death, and decay—the things that overcame the world against its will at God's command—will all disappear, and the world around us will share in the glorious freedom from sin which God's children enjoy.
    >
    > For we know that even the things of nature, like animals and plants, suffer in sickness and death as they await this great event.
    >
    > And ... we ... also groan to be released from pain and suffering. We too, wait anxiously for that day when God will give us our full rights as his children, including the new bodies he has promised us—bodies that will never be sick again and will never die.

16. Lewis, *The Problem of Pain*, op. cit., p. 70.
17. Thomas Hermiz, tape entitled "After You Have Suffered Awhile," given at Holiness Camp Meeting, Lakeland, Florida, February 18, 1983.

Chapter 6—Specific Causes of Suffering

1. Isaiah 14:12-15
2. Matthew 4:8-11
3. John 12:31; 14:30; 16:11; 2 Corinthians 4:4; Ephesians 2:2; 6:12; 1 John 5:19
4. Luke 22:53, TLB
5. John 19:11, NIV. See also Job 1:10-12; 2:6.
6. James 1:14
7. Judges 2:14,15
8. Joshua 7; Judges 10:6-8; 2 Kings 13:2,3; 17:19,20; 1 Chronicles 5:25,26; 10:13; 2 Chronicles 21:12-18
9. Though God may directly execute judgment for sin (1 Samuel 25:38; 1 Chronicles 2:3; 2 Chronicles 26:20; 32:21), more often He uses other people and natural disasters. For instance, He has used drought (1 Kings

16:33; 17:1), floods (Genesis 6–7), pestilence (2 Chronicles 7:13,14), storms (Jonah 1), or brimstone and fire (Genesis 13:12,13; 18:20–19:25). At other times He uses the heathen (1 Chronicles 10:3,13; 2 Chronicles 36:15-17). For example, Jeremiah 27:6 (TLB) describes Nebuchadnezzar of Babylon as God's "deputy." Many times God likewise used heathen kings without their knowledge (1 Kings 11:23; 2 Kings 13:2-4). However, "It is clear that these disasters befell Judah at the direct command of the Lord" (2 Kings 24:3,4, TLB). At other times He used godly men to execute His judgment (2 Samuel 12:1-14).

10. Genesis 38:7,10; Leviticus 10:1,2
11. Romans 14:10; Revelation 20:11-15

Chapter 7—God's Responsibility and Purpose in Suffering

1. Exodus 4:11
2. Joni Eareckson Tada and Steve Estes, *A Step Further* (New York: Bantam Books, 1987), p. 108.
3. Tozer, *The Knowledge of the Holy*, op. cit., p. 43, says: "The various elements of truth stand in perpetual antithesis, sometimes requiring opposites while we wait for the moment when we shall know as we are known. Then truth which now appears to be in conflict with itself will arise in shiny unity and it will be seen that the conflict has not been in the truth but in our sin-damaged minds."
4. Romans 8:28
5. Psalm 119:91, TLB
6. Genesis 50:20, TLB; see chapters 37–50.
7. Job 1:6-11, TLB
8. Hermiz, "After You Have Suffered Awhile," op. cit.
9. Frankl, *Man's Search for Meaning*, op. cit., pp. 121, 179.
10. 2 Thessalonians 1:4,5, TLB
11. Many people have misconceptions about Romans 8:28. It says that God will use everything in your life for good. Yet it also stipulates that one must love God and be called by Him in order for things to work together for good. The context makes it clear that the verse refers to "good" as viewed from God's perspective—the eternal perspective. This verse *does not say:*
    1) God causes all things.
    2) God wants everything to happen the way it does.
    3) God will work things together for good in a carnal Christian or non-Christian's life.
    4) A given event in itself is good.
    5) Any given event or situation will seem to work out for good immediately or even in this life.
    6) Things will work together for the Christian's comfort or pleasure and life will be easy.

    A more accurate translation of the Greek would be: "For it is God who is working all things together for the end of good, to those who are called according to His purpose."

12. Os Guinness, *In Two Minds* (Madison, WS: InterVarsity Press, 1976), p. 263.
13. Douglas D. Webster, *A Passion for Christ* (Grand Rapids, MI: Academic Books, 1987), p. 163.
14. Lewis, *The Problem of Pain*, op. cit., p. 81.
15. Howard Rutledge, *In the Presence of Mine Enemies* (Old Tappan, NJ: Revell, 1973), p. 34.
16. Job 36:15, TLB; see also Isaiah 42:25, TLB; Jeremiah 26:3-15; Hosea 5:15.
17. Genesis 6–7:1; Romans 2:5; See J.I. Packer's, *Knowing God* (Downers Grove, IL: InterVarsity Press, 1973), chapters 14–16, pp. 125-150. This deals with the fact that someone must atone for our sin.
18. John 3:16
19. 2 Peter 3:9, TLB; 1 Timothy 2:4; see also Genesis 6–7:1; Ezekiel 18:23; 33:11.
20. A number of passages remind us that we should expect suffering and that it will produce positive results in our lives: Deuteronomy 8:5; Romans 5:3-5; Hebrews 12:1-11; James 1:2-4,12; 1 Peter 4:12,13.
21. In my opinion, God does not need to create difficult circumstances for us just as a parent does not have to create situations in order to appropriately train his child. Plenty of situations occur by natural occurrences and God utilizes these to teach us and to develop desirable characteristics within us. Some well-meaning individuals would encourage seeking difficulty in order to grow. I frankly disagree with this position. If we truly follow God, plenty of stressful situations will naturally come our way. Matthew 6:34 remarks that today's troubles are sufficient without seeking any additional ones. The real question is whether or not we are utilizing current ones to the maximum.
22. Psalm 66:10; Isaiah 48:10,17; Zechariah 13:9; Malachi 3:2,3; 1 Peter 1:7
23. Some of the specific benefits of suffering are:
    a. It teaches us of His love and concern for us: Proverbs 3:11,12; Hebrews 12:5-9; Revelation 3:19
    b. It helps us keep His Word: Psalm 119:67-75
    c. It teaches us dependence and obedience: John 15:1-5; Hebrews 5:8
    d. It develops faith and trust in God: 1 Peter 1:3-7; 2 Corinthians 1:9,10
    e. It deepens our prayer life: Psalm 4:1; Isaiah 26:16
    f. It nurtures character and maturity: Romans 5:3-5; 1 Peter 5:8-10; James 1:2-4
    g. It produces perseverance and endurance: 2 Corinthians 4:8-18; James 1:2-4
    h. It cultivates righteousness in our lives: Hebrews 12:1-11
    i. It encourage hope: Romans 5:4; 2 Corinthians 4:8-17
    k. It enables us to bear more fruit: John 15:1-7
    l. We can be assured that God will ultimately reward the sufferer: James 1:12
24. 2 Corinthians 1:3,4, TLB
    How suffering can equip us to help others:
    a. It enables us to be an example to others in handling the inevitable difficulties of life: Hebrews 12:1-3

    b. It prepares us to be an authentic comfort to others: 2 Corinthians 1:3,4

    c. It helps bring others into a right relationship with God: Philippians 1:12-14

    d. Joni, a quadriplegic, says: "I was eventually to come to the conclusion that *one of God's purposes in increasing our trials is to sensitize us to people we never would have been able to relate to otherwise.*" Joni Eareckson and Steve Estes, *A Step Further,* op. cit., p. 5.

25. Job 2:9; 13:15, KJV; see also 1 Peter 1:6-13.

26. Lewis, *A Grief Observed*, op. cit., p. 25.

27. John 11:1-45, TLB; see also John 9:1-15; Romans 9:17.

28. Acts 6:5–8:1

29. William Byron Forbush, D.D. (ed.), *Foxe's Book of Martyrs* (Philadelphia: The John C. Winston Company, 1926).

30. John Bunyan, *The Pilgrims' Progress* (London: Letterworth Press, 1947).

31. Jeremiah 29:11-13, TLB

32. Understanding the cause of suffering: It is perfectly normal to want an answer to the question, "Why did this happen to me?" God doesn't mind the question. The search for a cause actually can help someone avoid adverse consequences and seek favorable ones. Occasionally I see a patient without any curiosity about why something has happened to him or her; and when offered a reason, even refuses to listen. Typically, this attitude brings greater problems. Understanding the causes clarifies the first step in removing the problem. Knowledge and understanding do not automatically cause appropriate action; a person has the responsibility to act. Nevertheless, the wisest actions generally grow out of the fullest possible understanding.

    On the other hand, the person must be willing to *accept* incomplete understanding of the cause. Often individuals refuse to accept the ambiguities of life. Sometimes, even when an answer is given, they refuse to accept it. Our mortality greatly limits our understanding, especially regarding suffering and misfortune. We can rebel at this incomplete understanding by blaming God, other people, or ourselves, or by taking up a never-ending, restless quest for more answers. The more mature person, though, will at some point accept incomplete understanding and gain peace of mind.

    The apostle Paul states in 2 Corinthians 4:8, (TLB) "We are perplexed because we don't know why things happen as they do, but we don't give up and quit." First Corinthians 13:12 (TLB) says, "In the same way, we can see and understand only a little about God now, as if we were peering at his reflection in a poor mirror; but some day we are going to see him in his completeness, face to face. Now all that I know is hazy and blurred, but then I will see everything clearly, just as clearly as God sees into my heart right now."

33. Scott Wesley Brown and Greg Nelson, "When Answers Aren't Enough." Copyright © 1986 Laurel Press (A division of Lorenz Creative Services, Pamela Kay Music—ASCAP); New Wings Music (A division of Lorenz Creative Services, and Greg Nelson Music—BMI). All rights reserved. Used by permission.

Chapter 8—Promises to Hold Onto

1. 1 John 1:9. See also Romans 8:1; James 5:13-15.
2. Psalm 105:13-17, TLB; Job 1:12; 2:6; John 19:11. See Lamentations 3:31-33; Isaiah 30:18-21. We are told, "For who can act against you without the Lord's permission?" (Lamentations 3:37, TLB; see also 4:11-13, TLB).

   Likewise, God always sets limits on how evil the unrighteous can be. At one point the Amorites were not quite evil enough for God to deal with them, but about 500 years later He commanded the Israelites to destroy them (Genesis 15:16; Leviticus 18:25). Also, when nations became as evil as Sodom and Gomorrah, He obliterated them (Genesis 19).

   2 Peter 2:5-9 (TLB) says:

   > And he did not spare any of the people who lived in ancient times before the flood except Noah, the one man who spoke up for God, and his family of seven. At that time God completely destroyed the whole world of ungodly men with the vast flood. Later, he turned the cities of Sodom and Gomorrah into heaps of ashes and blotted them off the face of the earth, making them an example for all the ungodly in the future to look back upon and fear.

   > But at the same time the Lord rescued Lot out of Sodom because he was a good man, sick of the terrible wickedness he saw everywhere around him day after day. So also the Lord can rescue you and me from the temptations that surround us, and continue to punish the ungodly until the day of final judgment comes.

3. 1 Corinthians 10:13; Psalm 103:10-14. God always shields His own. Jacob credited the Lord for the fact that Laban, though a dishonest employer, did not hurt him (Genesis 31:7). Satan, in fact, accused God of placing a hedge around Job so that he could not get to him. Even though God lifted that hedge in part, He still restricted Satan so that he could not take Job's life (Job 1–2). Pharaoh acted within definite limits beyond which he could not push the Israelites. King Saul could persecute David, but not to the point of taking his life. In the future tribulation, a time of persecution unlike any previous time, God affirms that He will limit those days for the sake of His chosen ones (Mark 13:19,20). God promises to keep us from premature harm (Isaiah 49:8,9, TLB).
4. Matthew 9:35,36. See also Psalm 4:1; Psalm 103:6-8; Matthew 7:7-11; 18:19; Mark 1:40-42; Mark 8:2,3; Luke 18:1-8; Hebrews 11.
5. Luke 12:4-7; Hebrews 13:5,6 TLB; see also Exodus 3:7-10; Psalm 23; 34:15-19; 37:28, TLB; 40:17; 41:3; 46:1,2; 112:1-8; 115:12; 139:17,18; Isaiah 30:20,21; 43:1-5; 46:3,4 TLB; 49:13-16; Jeremiah 29:11-13; 31:3; Romans 8:35-39; Ephesians 3:17-19; 1 Peter 5:7.

   Consider God's assurance to the following persons while they were going through affliction: Jacob (Genesis 28:15); Joseph (Genesis 39:21); Moses (Exodus 33:14); Paul (Acts 18:9,10; 23:11).
6. Matthew 1:23

> Men are nearly always longing for an easy religion, easy to understand and easy to follow; a religion with no mystery, no insoluble problems, no snags; a religion that would allow us to escape from our miserable human condition; a religion in which contact with God spares us all strife, all uncertainty, all suffering and all doubt, in short, a religion without the Cross. In the Bible, God does not take man out of his drama; but He lives it with him and for him.

Paul Tournier, *A Doctor's Casebook* (Westchester, IL: Good News Publishers), p. 6.

7. Paul Lindell, *The Mystery of Pain* (Minneapolis: Augsburg Publishing House, 1974), p. 39.
8. Romans 8:28; Genesis 50:20; John 11:4; Philippians 1:6
9. Revelation 2:9, TLB; Malachi 3:16,17; Romans 8:17-39; 2 Corinthians 4:15-18; Hebrews 12:11; James 4:14; 1 Peter 5:10
10. 1 Corinthians 13:9-12; Isaiah 55:6-9; John 13:7

Chapter 9—How God Heals

1. Adapted from editorial by Robert H. Moser, M.D., "Host Factors: An Overview," *Journal of American Medical Association*, May 5, 1975, Vol. 232, No. 5, pp. 516-519.
2. Tohru Ishigami, "The Influence of Psychic Acts on the Progress of Pulmonary Tuberculosis," *American Review of Tuberculosis*, 1919, Vol. 2, pp. 470-484.
3. As cited by Steven Locke, M.D., and Douglas Colligan, *The Healer Within* (New York: A Mentor Book, 1986), p. 69.
4. T. Holmes and R. Rahe, "The Social Readjustment Rating Scale," *Journal of Psychosomatic Research*, 1967, Vol. 11, pp. 213-218.
5. John Cassel, "The Contribution of the Social Environment to Host Resistance," *American Journal of Epidemiology*, February 1976, Vol. 104, No. 2, pp. 107-123.
6. The Scientific Board of the California Medical Association, "Epitomes—Important Advances in Clinical Medicine," *The Western Journal of Medicine*, July 1987, Vol. 147, No. 1, pp. 71-72; Marvin Stein, et al., "Stress and Immunomodulation: The Role of Depression and Neuroendocrine Function," *The Journal of Immunology*, August 1985, Vol. 135, No. 2, pp. 827-833; Robert M. Rose, M.D., "Endocrine Responses to Stressful Psychological Events," *Psychiatric Clinics of North America*, August 1980, Vol. 3, No. 2, pp. 251-276; Hugo O. Besedovsky, et al., "What do the Immune System and the Brain Know About Each Other?" *Immunology Today*, 1983, Vol. 4, No. 12, pp. 342-346.

A number of hormones have been found to be affected by stress and in turn affect the immune system. These include corticosteroids, catecholamines, growth hormone, prolactin, testosterone. In addition, a number of lymphocytes have been identified that play a direct role in surveillance and defending the individual against various infections and cancer. These cells include "Natural Killer Cells," B Cells, T Cells, etc.

7. Steven J. Schleifer, M.D., et al., "Suppression of Lymphocyte Stimulation Following Bereavement," *Journal of American Medical Association*, July 15, 1983, Vol. 250, No. 3, pp. 374-377; Michael Irwin, M.D., et al., "Life Events, Depressive Symptoms and Immune Function," *American Journal of Psychiatry*, April 1987, Vol. 144, No. 4, pp. 437-441; Steven J. Schleifer, M.D., et al., "Lymphocyte Function in Major Depressive Disorder," *Archives of General Psychiatry*, May 1984, Vol. 41, pp. 474-486; Suzanne C. Kobasa, et al., "Personality and Constitution as Mediators in the Stress-Illness Relationship," *Journal of Health and Social Behavior*, December 1981, Vol. 22, pp. 368-378; Jerome K. Myers, Ph.D., et al., "Life Events and Psychiatric Impairment," *The Journal of Nervous and Mental Disease*, March 1971, Vol. 152, No. 3, pp. 149-157; Janice K. Kiecolt-Glaser, Ph.D., Ronald Glaser, Ph.D., "Psychological Influences on Immunity," *Psychosomatics*, September 1986, Vol. 27, No. 9, pp. 621-624; Steven F. Maier, Mark Laudenslager, "Stress and Health: Exploring the Links," *Psychology Today*, August 1985, pp. 44-49.

8. Robert Ornstein, Ph.D., and David Sobel, Ph.D., *The Healing Brain* (New York: Simon & Schuster, 1987), p. 26.

9. Proverbs 17:22

10. Ornstein and Sobel, *The Healing Brain*, op. cit., chapter 4; James M. George, Ph.D., Donald S. Scott, Ph.D., "The Effects of Psychological Factors on Recovery from Surgery," *Journal of American Dental Association*, August 1982, Vol. 105, pp. 251-258; Howard R. Hall, Ph.D., "Hypnosis and the Immune System: A Review with Implications for Cancer and the Psychology of Healing," *American Journal of Clinical Hypnosis*, October 1982-January 1983, Vol. 25, Nos. 2-3, pp. 92-103.

11. Norman Cousins, *Anatomy of an Illness: As Perceived by the Patient* (New York: W.W. Norton & Co., 1979).

12. O. Carl Simonton, M.D., et al., "Psychological Intervention in the Treatment of Cancer," *Psychosomatics*, March 1980, Vol. 21, No. 3, pp. 226-233.

13. Steven E. Locke, M.D., et al., "Life Change Stress, Psychiatric Symptoms, and Natural Killer Cell Activity," *Psychosomatic Medicine*, September/October 1984, Vol. 46, No. 5, pp. 441-453; Janice Kiecolt-Glaser and Ronald Glaser, "Psychological Influences on Immunity," *Psychosomatics*, September 1986, Vol. 27, No. 9, pp. 621-624; Katherine Nuckolls, et al., "Psychosocial Assets, Life Crisis and the Prognosis of Pregnancy," *The American Journal of Epidemiology*, 1972, Vol. 95, No. 5, pp. 431-441.

14. Janice K. Keicolt-Glaser, Ph.D., et al. "Psychosocial Modifiers of Immunocompetence in Medical Students," *Psychosomatic Medicine*, January/February 1984, Vol. 46, No. 1, pp. 7-14; Ziad Kronfol, et al., "Impaired Lymphocyte Function in Depressive Illness," *Life Sciences*, 1983, Vol. 33, pp. 241-247; Steven J. Schleifer, M.D., et al., "Suppression of Lymphocyte Stimulation Following Bereavement," *Journal of American Medical Association*, July 15, 1983, Vol. 250, No. 3, pp. 374-377; Michael Irwin, et al., "Life Events, Depressive Symptoms, and Immune Function," *American Journal of Psychiatry*, April 1987, Vol. 144, No. 4, pp. 437-441.

15. How you live may affect how long you live. For years I have heard the statement, "When your time is up, that's it." However, by carefully

reading the Scriptures, I have come to believe that how someone lives may affect not only the quality of his life but also the length of life. Obviously, if God firmly sets the limit of a given person's life, there is very little that he can do to alter it. In certain instances, I believe that time is firmly set. Also, if we live in the last days, the Lord's return will determine how long many of us remain on this earth. However, for most people I believe the Lord has set in motion normal laws of life and disease. "As for the days of our life, they contain seventy years, or if due to strength, eighty years..." (Psalm 90:10). If a person takes care of himself physically, emotionally, and spiritually, he may add some years to his life (1 Kings 3:14). "The fear of the Lord prolongs life, but the years of the wicked will be shortened" (Proverbs 10:27). Similarly, God promises a long life to those who honor their parents (Exodus 20:12). On the other hand, abuse of his body may shorten someone's life. First Corinthians 11:30 (TLB) tells us that inappropriately partaking of the Sacrament of Communion caused premature sickness and suffering. It says, "That is why many of you are weak and sick, and some have even died." Psalm 78:32,33 (TLB) relates, "The people kept on sinning... so he cut their lives short and gave them years of terror and disaster." Moses died prematurely because in his anger he disobeyed God (Deuteronomy 32:48-51). Hezekiah, on the other hand, prayed and God heard him and replied, "I will add fifteen years to your life..." (2 Kings 20:1-6).

16. William A. Nolan, M.D., *Healing: A Doctor in Search of a Miracle* (New York: Random House, 1976), p. 272.

17. *Webster's New Collegiate Dictionary* (Springfield, MA: G.& C. Merriam Company, 1953), p. 537.

18. The editor interviews Warren H. Cole, M.D., "Spontaneous Regression of Cancer," *Cancer—A Cancer Journal for Clinicians*, September/October 1974, Vol. 24, No. 5, pp. 274-279.

19. Harvey W. Baker, M.D., "Biologic Control of Cancer," *Archives of Surgery*, November 1986, Vol. 121, pp. 1237-1241.

    An example of some of the reports:

    L. Herbert Maurer, M.D., et al., "Spontaneous Regression of Malignant Melanoma: Pathologic and Immunologic Study in a Ten Year Survivor," *The American Journal of Surgery*, April 1974, Vol. 127, pp. 397-403; Ben M. Birkhead, M.D., and Ralph M. Scott, M.D., "Spontaneous Regression of Metastatic Testicular Cancer," *Cancer*, July 1973, Vol. 32, pp. 125-129.

20. Charles Weinstock, "Recent Progress in Cancer Psychobiology and Psychiatry," *Journal of the American Society of Psychosomatic Dentistry and Medicine*, 1977, Vol. 24, No. 1, pp. 4-14; Charles Weinstock, "Notes on 'Spontaneous' Regression of Cancer," *Journal of the American Society of Psychosomatic Dentistry and Medicine*, 1977, Vol. 24, No. 4, pp. 106-110.

21. Bernie S. Siegel, M.D., *Love, Medicine & Miracles* (New York: Harper & Row Publishers, 1986), p. 21.

22. John 9; John 11

23. John 5:2-16, see also John 9:3.

24. John 14:11, NIV
25. Matthew 9:6
26. Exodus 9:14, TLB
27. John 6:26
28. David Watson, *Fear No Evil* (Wheaton, IL: Harold Shaw Publishers, 1984), p. 52.
29. Luke 10:20
30. John 20:29
31. Milton W. Kohut, "Lord, Why Me?" *World Vision*, July 1979, p. 19. Hosea 11:3 says, "But they did not know that I healed them."
32. Siegel, *Love, Medicine & Miracles*, op. cit., p. 214.
33. Mark 3:22
34. James 1:17, NIV

Chapter 10—Face Your Feelings

1. I have heard the story of the experiment of the man giving out $100 bills several times. Though I cannot authenticate the experiment, it certainly is true of life. I have seen it in print in *Faith Is Not A Feeling* by Ney Bailey (San Bernardino, CA: Here's Life Publishers, Inc., 1978), pp. 57-59.
2. 2 Corinthians 4:8
3. Psalm 42:3; 43:5, TLB
4. Leonard R. Derogatis, Ph.D., et al., "Psychological Coping Mechanisms and Survival Time in Metastatic Breast Cancer," *Journal of the American Medical Association*, October 5, 1979, Vol. 242, No. 14, pp. 1504-1508.
5. S. Greer and Tina Morris, "Psychological Attributes of Women Who Develop Breast Cancer: A Controlled Study," *Journal of Psychosomatic Research*, 1975, Vol. 19, pp. 147-153.
6. Elisabeth Kubler-Ross, *On Death and Dying* (New York: MacMillan, 1969).
7. Mara Julius, et al., "Anger-Coping Types, Blood Pressure, and All-Cause Mortality: A Follow-up in Tecumseh, Michigan," *American Journal of Epidemiology*, 1986, Vol. 124, No. 2, pp. 220-233.
8. For a detailed discussion on the subject of constructively handling your hurts and anger see *Overcoming Hurts and Anger* by Dwight L. Carlson, M.D. (Eugene, OR: Harvest House Publishers, 1981).
9. See *Guilt Free*, Dwight L. Carlson, M.D. (Eugene, OR: Harvest House Publishers, 1983).
10. Philippians 4:6
11. 2 Corinthians 11:28, TLB; John 12:27, TLB
12. 1 Kings 19; Psalm 22:1,2; Job 10
13. Watson, *Fear No Evil*, op. cit., pp. 48-49.
14. 2 Timothy 4:11; 2 Corinthians 1:8,9; Psalm 10:1, NIV; Matthew 27:46
15. Hermiz, "After You Have Suffered Awhile," op. cit.
16. Thielicke, *Out of the Depths*, op. cit., p. 15.
17. Robert L. Veninga, *A Gift of Hope: How We Survive Our Tragedies* (New York: Ballantine Books, 1985), p. 133.
18. John White, *The Fight* (Downers Grove, IL: InterVarsity Press, 1976), pp. 106-107.

19. Quoted by Viktor E. Frankl, *The Unconscious God* (New York: Simon and Schuster, 1975), p. 126.
20. Thomas R. Kelly, *A Testament of Devotion* (New York: Harper & Brothers, 1941), p. 10.
21. "Endocrine Responses to Stressful Psychological Events," *Psychiatric Clinics of North America*, August 1980, Vol. 3, No. 2, pp. 251-276; Captain Richard H. Rahe, Mc USN, "Life Change Events and Mental Illness: An Overview," *Journal of Human Stress*, September 1979, Vol. 5, No. 3, pp. 2-10.
22. Frankl, *Man's Search for Meaning*, op. cit., pp. 103-105, 178, 213.
23. Hebrews 12:11
24. Watson, *Fear No Evil*, op. cit., p. 133.
25. Thielicke, *Out of the Depths*, op. cit., p. 41.

Chapter 11—Seek Appropriate Help

1. James 5:13-15
2. Matthew 8:4
3. Parker, *We Let Our Son Die*, op. cit., p. 165.
4. 1 Corinthians 12:9
5. Daniel 3:17,18
6. James 5:13-15; Mark 6:13
7. John 9:6,7; Isaiah 38:21, NIV; 1 Timothy 5:23
8. Thomas P. Hackett, M.D., et al., "Patient Delay in Cancer," *New England Journal of Medicine*, July 5, 1973, Vol. 289, No. 1, pp. 14-20.
9. Anthony Reading, "The Effects of Psychological Preparation on Pain and Recovery after Minor Gynecological Surgery: A Preliminary Report," *Journal of Clinical Psychology*, 1982, Vol. 38, No. 3, pp. 504-512.
10. P.M. West, et al., "An Observed Correlation Between Psychological Factors and Growth Rate of Cancer in Man," *Cancer Research*, 1952, Vol. 12, p. 306.
11. Siegel, *Love, Medicine & Miracles*, op. cit., pp. 3, 51.

Chapter 12—The Will to Health

1. Cassell, *The Healer's Art*, op. cit., p. 44.
2. Suzanne C. Kobasa, et al., "Hardiness and Health; A Prospective Study," *Journal of Personality and Social Psychology*, 1982, Vol. 42, No. 1, pp. 168-177.
3. Suzanne C. Kobasa, "Stressful Life Events, Personality, and Health: An Inquiry Into Hardiness," *Journal of Personality and Social Psychology*, January 1979, Vol. 37, No. 1, pp. 1-11.
4. Ornstein and Sobel, *The Healing Brain*, op. cit., p. 157; P.M. West, "An Observer's Correlation" op. cit., p. 306; Sandra M. Levy, "Emotions and The Progression of Cancer: A Review," *Advances*, Winter 1984, Vol. 1, No. 1, pp. 10-15.
5. Psalm 8:6, TLB. See also Exodus 32; 1 Samuel 3:10–4:11; 2 Kings 20:1-3; Luke 18:1-8.
6. Karen Gravelle, "Can a Feeling of Capability Reduce Arthritis Pain?" *Advances*, Summer 1985, Vol. 2, No. 3, pp. 8-13.
7. Siegel, *Love, Medicine & Miracles*, op. cit., jacket.

8. Cousins, *Anatomy of an Illness*, op. cit., p. 11.
9. Judith Rodin and Ellen J. Langer, "Long-Term Effects of a Control-Relevant Intervention with the Institutionalized Aged," *Journal of Personality and Social Psychology*, 1977, Vol. 35, No. 12, pp. 897-902.

Chapter 13—We Really Need Each Other

1. Ruttledge, *In the Presence of Mine Enemies*, op. cit., p. 41.
2. Segal, *Winning Life's Toughest Battles*, op. cit., chapter 1.
3. Derogatis, "Psychological Coping Mechanisms," op. cit., pp. 1504-1508.
4. Janice K. Kiecolt-Glaser, Ph.D., et al., "Urinary Cortisol Levels, Cellular Immunocompetency, and Loneliness in Psychiatric Inpatients," *Psychosomatic Medicine*, Jan./Feb. 1984, Vol. 46, No. 1, pp. 15-23; Janice K. Kiecolt-Glaser, Ph.D., et al., "Psychosocial Modifiers of Immunocompetence in Medical Students," *Psychosomatic Medicine*, Jan./Feb. 1984, Vol. 46, No. 1, pp. 7-14.
5. Lisa F. Berkman, and S. Leonard Syme, "Social Networks, Host Resistance, and Mortality: A Nine-Year Follow-up of Alameda County Residents," *American Journal of Epidemiology*, 1979, Vol. 109, No. 2, pp. 186-204; Lisa F. Berkman, "Assessing the Physical Health Effects of Social Networks and Social Support," *Annual Review of Public Health*, 1984, Vol. 5, pp. 413-432.
6. Erika Friedmann, Ph.D., et al., "Animal Companions and One-Year Survival of Patients After Discharge From A Coronary Care Unit," *Public Health Reports*, July/Aug. 1980, Vol. 95, No. 4, pp. 307-312; Faith T. Fitzgerald, M.A., "The Therapeutic Value of Pets [commentary]," *The Western Journal of Medicine*, January 1986, Vol. 144, No. 1, pp. 103-105.
7. Leon Eisenberg, M.D., "A Friend, Not an Apple, A Day Will Help Keep the Doctor Away," *The American Journal of Medicine*, April 1979, Vol. 66, pp. 551-553.
8. Hebrews 10:25

Chapter 14—To Accept the Things I Cannot Change

1. Philip Yancey, *Where Is God When It Hurts?* (Grand Rapids, MI: The Zondervan Corporation, 1977), pp. 107-108 (see chapter 8). Used by permission.
2. 2 Corinthians 12:7-10; Matthew 26:38-42; Galatians 4:13-15; 2 Timothy 4:20
3. Ornstein and Sobel, *The Healing Brain*, op. cit., p. 36.
4. Locke and Colligan, *The Healer Within*, op. cit., p. 195; Barrie R. Cassileth, et al., "Psychosocial Correlates of Survival in Advanced Malignant Disease?" *The New England Journal of Medicine*, June 13, 1985, Vol. 312, No. 24, pp. 1551-1555; Lynn Smith, "Mind Over Body: Doubt Rekindled," *Los Angeles Times*, August 20, 1985, Part 1, pp. 1-16.
5. M. Scott Peck, M.D., *The Road Less Traveled* (New York: Simon and Schuster, 1978), p. 15.
6. Catherine Marshall, *Beyond Ourselves* (New York: Avon Books, 1961), p. 130.
7. Ruttledge, *In the Presence of Mine Enemies*, op. cit., p. 64.

Chapter 15—The Healing Power of Hope

1. Romans 8:24,25

2. Rose F. McGee, R.N., Ph.D., quotes S.M. Vaillot in "Hope: A Factor Influencing Crisis Resolution," *Advances in Nursing Science*, July 1984, pp. 34-44; Judith Fitzgerald Miller quotes Gabriel Marcel, "Inspiring Hope," *American Journal of Nursing*, January 1985, pp. 22-25.
3. Robert Mills, "An Anatomy of Hope," *Journal of Religion and Health*, 1979, Vol. 18, No. 1.
4. Locke and Colligan quote Joel Dimsdale, psychiatrist, in *The Healer Within*, op. cit., p. 220.
5. William M. Buchholz, M.D., "The Medical Uses of Hope," *The Western Journal of Medicine*, January 1988, Vol. 148, p. 69. Reprinted by permission of the *Western Journal of Medicine*.
6. Daniel Goleman, Ph.D., quotes Norman Cousins in "Denial & Hope," *American Health*, December 1984, pp. 54-59.
7. This experiment is related by Chuck Smith, Pastor of Calvary Chapel, Bible study tape #1846, Romans 8:24,25, "The Word for Today," Costa Mesa, CA, 1976.
8. Segal, *Winning Life's Toughest Battles*, op. cit., p. 97.
9. Ornstein and Sobel, *The Healing Brain*, op. cit., p. 243.
10. McGee quotes E. Stotland in "Hope," op. cit.
11. John Bruhn, "Therapeutic Value of Hope," *Southern Medical Journal*, February 1984, Vol. 77, No. 2, pp. 215-219.
12. E. Stanley Jones, excerpt from the "Divine Yes," *Eternity Magazine*, February 1975.
13. Hosea 2:15, TLB
14. Psalm 27:13
15. E. James Anthony, Bertram J. Cohler (eds.), *The Invulnerable Child* (New York: The Guilford Press, 1987), p. 103.
16. Segal, *Winning Life's Toughest Battles*, op. cit., p. 95.
17. Veninga, *A Gift of Hope*, op. cit., pp. 279, 88.
18. Ornstein and Sobel, *The Healing Brain*, op. cit., p. 113.
19. Hebrews 6:19,20
20. Tozer, *The Knowledge of the Holy*, op. cit., pp. 10-11.
21. Romans 8:18, KJV; 2 Corinthians 4:17,18, KJV. See also Isaiah 25:7,8; Isaiah 65:17; Revelation 7:14-17; Revelation 21:4.

Chapter 16—Laughter, Praise, and Joy

1. Lee F. Tuttle, *Profiles of 20th Century Pulpit Giants*, is quoted by Donald E. Demaray, p. 105 in *Laughter, Joy, and Healing* (Grand Rapids, MI: Baker Books, 1986), p. 76. Twenty-four preachers were evaluated and found to have characteristics common to all, "but perhaps a sense of humor was the most unanimously a major [feature]."
2. E. James Anthony and Bertram J. Cohler (eds.), *The Invulnerable Child*, op. cit., p. 100.
3. John G. Bruhn, Ph.D., quotes A. Burton in "Therapeutic Value of Hope," *Southern Medical Journal*, February 1984, Vol. 77, No. 2, pp. 215-216.
4. Cousins, *Anatomy of an Illness*, op. cit., p. 39; Frankl, *Man's Search for Meaning*, op. cit., p. 68; Demaray, *Laughter, Joy, and Healing*, op. cit., p. 105;

Proverbs 17:22, NIV; Kathleen M. Dillon, Ph.D., et al., "Positive Emotional States and Enhancement of the Immune System," *International Journal of Psychiatry in Medicine*, 1985-1986, Vol. 15, No. 1 , pp. 13-17.

5. Nehemiah 8:10

Chapter 17—Suffering with Purpose and Meaning

1. Brother Lawrence, The *Practice of the Presence of God* (Old Tappan, NJ: Spire Books, 1958), p. 62.
2. Frankl, *Man's Search for Meaning*, op. cit., p. 179.
3. Suzanne C. Kobasa, et al., quotes A. Antonovsky, in "Hardiness and Health: A Prospective Study," *Journal of Personality and Social Psychology*, 1982, Vol. 42, No. 1, p. 168; Kobasa, ibid., pp. 168-177; Suzanne C. Kobasa, "Stressful Life Events, Personality, and Health: An Inquiry into Hardiness, "*Journal of Personality and Social Psychology*, January 1979, Vol. 37, No. 1, pp. 1-11.
4. Locke and Colligan, *The Healer Within*, op. cit., p. 220.
5. James M. George, Ph.D., and Donald S. Scott, Ph.D., "The Effects of Psychological Factors on Recovery From Surgery," *Journal of American Dental Association*, August 1982, Vol. 105, pp. 251-258.
6. Frankl, *Man's Search for Meaning*, op. cit., pp. 106-107.
7. 2 Corinthians 1:3,4
8. Oswald Chambers, *Baffled to Fight Better*, op. cit., p. 20.
9. 2 Corinthians 12:9,10
10. James 1:2,3: "Consider it all joy, my brethren, when you encounter various trials, knowing that the testing of your faith produces endurance." 1 Thessalonians 5:16-18: "Rejoice always; pray without ceasing; in everything give thanks; for this is God's will for you in Christ Jesus."
11. Thielicke, *Out of the Depths*, op. cit., pp. 14-15.
12. Margaret Clarkson, *Destined for Glory* (Grand Rapids, MI: Eerdmans Publishing Company, 1983), p. 113.
13. Genesis 50:20, NIV
14. Frankl, *Man's Search for Meaning*, op. cit., p. 183.

Appendix—How to Help a Friend Who Is Hurting

1. Ecclesiastes 3:1, NIV
2. Proverbs 25:11
3. John 11:1-45
4. Shawn Strannigan, "You Can Comfort Those Who Mourn," *Partnership*, Sept./Oct. 1986, p. 41. A publication of Christianity Today, Inc., Carol Stream, Illinois.
5. Merrill and Virginia Womach, *Tested by Fire* (Old Tappan, NJ: Fleming H. Revell Company, 1976), pp. 23-24.
6. Joni Eareckson, *Joni* (Grand Rapids, MI: Zondervan Publishing House, 1976), p. 55.
7. Beth Austin, "Showing Compassion to Grieving Parents," *American Medical News*, October 10, 1986, p. 15.
8. Proverbs 14:10, TLB
9. Cassell, *The Healer's Art*, op. cit., p. 198.

10. Frankl, *Man's Search for Meaning*, op. cit., p. 53.
11. Proverbs 25:20, TLB
12. John G. Gunderson, M.D., "Patient-Therapist Matching: A Research Evaluation," *American Journal of Psychiatry*, October 1978, Vol. 135, pp. 1193-1197.
13. Ecclesiastes 1:18
14. Robert M. Rose, M.D., "Endocrine Responses to Stressful Psychological Events," *Psychiatric Clinics of North America*, 1980, Vol. 3, No. 2, pp. 251-276; Thomas P. Hackett, M.D., et al., "The Coronary-Care Unit, An Appraisal of Its Psychologic Hazards," *The New England Journal of Medicine*, December 19, 1968, Vol. 279, No. 25, pp. 1365-1370; Richard S. Lazarus, interviewed by Daniel Goleman, "Positive Denial: The Case for Not Facing Reality," *Psychology Today*, November 1979, pp. 44-60.
15. Roberto Sosa, M.D., et al., "The Effect of a Supportive Companion on Perinatal Problems, Length of Labor, and Mother-Infant Interaction," *The New England Journal of Medicine*, September 11, 1980, Vol. 303, No. 11, pp. 597-600.
16. Eugene W. Broadhead, et al., "The Epidemiologic Evidence for a Relationship Between Social Support and Health," *American Journal of Epidemiology*, May 1983, Vol. 117, No. 5, pp. 521-537.
17. Lisa F. Berkman, "Assessing the Physical Health Effects of Social Networks and Social Support," *Annual Review of Public Health*, 1984, Vol. 5, pp. 413-432.
18. Carolyn Coil, "In Sympathy," *The Daily Breeze*, February 5, 1984, C1.
19. Joseph Bayly, *The Last Thing We Talk About* (Elgin, IL: David C. Cook Publishing Company, 1973), pp. 55-56.
20. Chambers, *Baffled to Fight Better*, op. cit., p. 33.

Appendix—Applying Healing Principles

1. Veninga, *A Gift of Hope*, op. cit., p. 278.

Recommended Reading

**The following books are excellent
on the subject of suffering:**

Clarkson, Margaret, *Grace Grows Best in Winter*, Zondervan, 1972. This is an excellent book for a person suffering with a chronic illness.

_____ . *Destined for Glory*, Zondervan, 1983. This book will help give understanding of the problem as well as comfort. Margaret Clarkson writes from her own experience with suffering.

Eareckson, Joni, *Joni*, Zondervan, 1976. An outstanding book on her struggle as a quadriplegic with depression.

Eareckson, Joni and Estes, Steve, *A Step Further*, Zondervan, 1978.

Hopkins, Hugh Evan, *The Mystery of Suffering*, InterVarsity, 1959. An excellent general book on suffering.

Lewis, C.S., *A Grief Observed*, Bantam Books, 1976. This is about Lewis' rediscovered faith after a severe loss.

_____ . *The Problem of Pain*, Macmillan, New York, 1961. A classic book for those who want to delve deeply into this subject.

Rutledge, Howard and Phyllis with White, Mel and Lyla, *In the Presence of Mine Enemies*, Revell, 1973. A moving account of Howard's seven years as a prisoner of war in a North Vietnamese prison.

Segal, Dr. Julius, *Winning Life's Toughest Battles: Roots of Human Resilience*, Ivy Books, 1986. This is an excellent secular book about ingredients that helped prisoners and hostages to survive against tremendous odds.

Veninga, Robert L., *A Gift of Hope: How We Survive Our Tragedies*, Ballantine Books, 1985. A very good book dealing with surviving in the face of tragedies and the value of hope.

Weatherhead, Leslie D., *The Will of God*, Abingdon Press, 1944. An outstanding short paperback on God's various wills, written during World War II.

Wise, Robert L., *When There Is No Miracle*, Regal Books, 1977. This will be an excellent book for the suffering person who has not experienced a miraculous intervention.

Womach, Merrill and Virginia with White, Mel and Lyla, *Tested by Fire*, Revell, 1976. This excellent book describes the aftermath of an airplane crash, the suffering that followed with the numerous surgeries—all taken very gallantly.

Yancey, Philip, *Where is God When it Hurts?*, Zondervan, 1977. One of the best books on the subject.

Other books on the subject of suffering:

Baker, Don, *Pain's Hidden Purpose*, Multnomah Press, 1983. This addresses maintaining perspective in suffering.

Claypool, John, *Tracks of a Fellow Struggler*, Word, 1974. A very good book for someone who has just lost a loved one.

Frankl, Viktor E., *Man's Search for Meaning*, Washington Square Press, 1959. This was written by a Jewish psychiatrist who spent several years in a Nazi concentration camp. Though not from a Christian perspective, there is a lot of meaningful material that is very applicable to anyone suffering.

Kubler-Ross, Elisabeth, *On Death and Dying*, Macmillan, 1969. A classic book on death and dying from the secular perspective.

Kushner, Harold S., *When Bad Things Happen to Good People*, Avon, 1981. This book, written by a Jewish rabbi, contains a lot of excellent material. It falls short, though, in that it leaves Christ out of the picture and essentially portrays God as impotent.

Landorf, Joyce, *Mourning Song*, Revell, 1974. As Joyce's mother was dying, Joyce writes that her mother had taught her about life and had not wanted to teach her about dying. What Joyce "learned" is shared in this book.

Lindell, Paul J., *The Mystery of Pain*, Augsburg Publishing House, 1974. A basic book on the subject of suffering.

Locke, Steven, M.D., and Colligan, Douglas, *The Healer Within, the New Medicine of Mind and Body*, A Mentor Book, 1987. This is a very good secular book discussing the body's capabilities of healing.

Matthews, A.J., *Why Me?*, Christian Literature Crusade, 1972. A basic book on the subject of suffering.

Ornstein, Robert and Sobel, David, *The Healing Brain*, Simon & Schuster, 1987. This is a well-written book on the ability of the mind in aiding the healing process. My only reservation is the authors' bent toward evolution.

Schaeffer, Edith, *Affliction*, Revell, 1978.

Schaper, Robert N., *Why Me, God?*, Regal Books, 1974. An excellent study of the Book of Job as it relates to suffering.

Tengbom, Mildred, *Why Waste Your Illness?*, Augsburg, 1984. Some good thoughts regarding trying to make the most of suffering.

Westberg, Granger E., *Good Grief*, Fortress Press, 1962. This is a good little book that covers the basic process of grief.

Woods, B.W., *Understanding Suffering*, Baker Book House, 1974. A basic but, I believe, accurate book on the subject.

Other Good
Harvest House Reading

OVERCOMING HURTS AND ANGER
by *Dr. Dwight Carlson*

Dr. Carlson shows us how to confront our feelings and negative emotions in order to experience liberation and fulfillment. He presents seven practical steps to help us identify and cope with our feelings of hurt and anger.

GOD'S BEST FOR MY LIFE
by *Lloyd John Ogilvie*

Not since Oswald Chambers' *My Utmost for His Highest* has there been such an inspirational yet easy-to-read devotional. Dr. Ogilvie provides guidelines for maximizing your prayer and meditation time.

LORD, I'VE GOT A PROBLEM
by *Don Baker*

Don Baker, bestselling author of *Beyond Forgiveness* takes on a number of the most common problems that *every* person faces. Through the eyes of a knowledgeable and sensitive counselor, Don works through the dilemmas of life and gives not only his own remarkable insight, but thoroughly explains biblical solutions that will equip you for the struggles of life.

THE FATHER HEART OF GOD
by *Floyd McClung Jr.*

The Father Heart of God is a book about the healing power of God's love. In its pages you'll discover how the loving, compassionate Father Heart of God enables us to overcome insecurity and the devastating effects of some of life's most painful experiences.

STORMIE
by *Stormie Omartian*

The childhood of singer/songwriter Stormie Omartian, marred by physical and emotional abuse, led into teen and adult years filled with tragedy. Searching for an end to the inner turmoil which constantly confronted her, Stormie found herself on the verge of suicide. In this poignant story there is help and hope for anyone who doubts the value of his or her own life. It gloriously reveals a God who can bring life out of death if we are willing to surrender to His ways.

HOW TO WIN OVER WORRY
by *John Haggai*

People need help in overcoming worry and need it desperately. The worry problem is at the root of much domestic strife, business failure, economic crises, incurable sicknesses, and premature deaths—to mention but a few of worry's hazards. Presenting more than a diagnosis, Dr. Haggai shows how God's Word offers the prescription for worry that can rid us of the devastating effects of worry forever.

THE QUIET HEART
by *June Masters Bacher*

In this all-new devotional by June Masters Bacher, each daily devotional begins with a suggested Scripture reading, and through anecdotes, poetry, and prayer inspires each reader to see life with a fresh perspective. A day-by-day "friend" that encourages a quiet heart so you can come to know God and learn how much richer knowing Him makes each day.

Dear Reader:

We would appreciate hearing from you regarding this Harvest House nonfiction book. It will enable us to continue to give you the best in Christian publishing.

1. What most influenced you to purchase *When Life Isn't Fair?*
   - ☐ Author
   - ☐ Subject matter
   - ☐ Backcover copy
   - ☐ Recommendations
   - ☐ Cover/Title
   - ☐ _____

2. Where did you purchase this book?
   - ☐ Christian bookstore
   - ☐ General bookstore
   - ☐ Department store
   - ☐ Grocery store
   - ☐ Other

3. Your overall rating of this book:
   ☐ Excellent ☐ Very good ☐ Good ☐ Fair ☐ Poor

4. How likely would you be to purchase other books by this author?
   - ☐ Very likely
   - ☐ Somewhat likely
   - ☐ Not very likely
   - ☐ Not at all

5. What types of books most interest you?
   (check all that apply)
   - ☐ Women's Books
   - ☐ Marriage Books
   - ☐ Current Issues
   - ☐ Self Help/Psychology
   - ☐ Bible Studies
   - ☐ Fiction
   - ☐ Biographies
   - ☐ Children's Books
   - ☐ Youth Books
   - ☐ Other _____

6. Please check the box next to your age group.
   - ☐ Under 18
   - ☐ 18-24
   - ☐ 25-34
   - ☐ 35-44
   - ☐ 45-54
   - ☐ 55 and over

Mail to: Editorial Director
Harvest House Publishers
1075 Arrowsmith
Eugene, OR 97402

Name _____

Address _____

City _____ State _____ Zip _____

Thank you for helping us to help you in future publications!